Fast Patch

Other books available from Chilton:

Fast Patch

A Treasury of Strip-Quilt Projects

Anita Hallock

Chilton Book Company
Radnor, Pennsylvania

Published in Radnor, Pennsylvania 19089, by Chilton Book Company

Color pages designed by Kevin Culver

Color photography by Walter A. Biddle

Designed by Martha Vercoutere

Illustrations by Anita Hallock

Manufactured in the United States of America

LC #89-42855

ISBN 0-8019-8004-6

1 2 3 4 5 6 7 8 9 0   8 7 6 5 4 3 2 1 0 9

To Lillie Scherler

Table of Contents

Introduction

Quiltmaking endures because it's relaxing and after you're done there's such a satisfying sense of accomplishment. But let's face it, some of us have less time to relax in than others, and we need to get our glow of pride right away or we'll be stuck with the guilt of half-finished projects instead.

The invention of the wheel

Many of us would still be admiring quilts, or dreaming of them, but not making them ourselves, if it hadn't been for the invention of the wheel—in this case the wheel cutter. With the rotary cutter and the new strip-piecing techniques, we got just enough high technology to remove the tedium from quiltmaking. We can still make the sentimental old designs, but we can make them faster now.

We no longer have to feel guilty if slow, patient work doesn't meet our needs. Personally, I need a technique which is fast and interesting, makes traditional American blocks, and is practical, so I can enjoying using the quilts when they're finished.

Fast Patch is born

In 1983 I developed a new strip technique for making triangles, and that made all of those things possible. In 1984 I chose the name Fast Patch.

In 1985 I started teaching Adult Ed. students at Lane Community College, and Jenny Falknor got me started with the Macintosh computer. In 1986 Del and Marlene Matheson and Lillie Scherler helped publish my first books, and quilt shops started selling them. By 1987, with another boost from Hans and Stephanie Weisenfarth, we had seven small books in print. In 1988 we discovered Walt Biddle and added color photographs. In 1989 Robbie Fanning invited me to have Chilton publish the books. Folks around the country sent projects to me on short notice so Walt could do the slides for this book, and Alice Bloomer and Dorsy Hancock shared their homes and antiques. Thank you to all those special people. Thank you, also, to my husband, George, who is instrumental in running our business; and our children, who always know where they can find me, but can't always get me to come out and cook a meal or sew on a button.

Much of the material in this book has been compiled from four of our early books, but there are a lot of new ideas too. Fast Patch has changed forever a lot of people's ideas about patchwork quilts. I hope you enjoy it too.

Anita Hallock
Springfield, Oregon

How to use this book

This book has enough projects and ideas to last a lifetime. But not all the ideas are for you, at least not this week.

Please look through the whole book before starting a project. Which parts should you study thoroughly and which can you skim over? Which projects should you try first? Let me suggest these five steps:

Steps 1 and 2 depend on your experience.

If you haven't made many quilts:

1. Read Chapter 1 thoroughly. Get your tools and practice cutting strips.

2. Make at least one project from Chapter 2.

If you want to spend years doing projects in Chapter 2, that's fine. With every project, you get better at choosing colors, using the rotary cutter, and doing basic patchwork. Do you have to finish up every project, quilt it, and bind it? No. Most folks sew for fun, not because they need more bedding.

If you've made quilts, but not with the rotary cutter and not with strips:

1. Read pages 5, 6, and 7 thoroughly. There are some fabric restrictions when sewing with strips, and you do need the special tools. Skim over the rest of Chapter 1.

2. Make at least one project from Chapter 2 using the rotary cutter.

Do these projects seem simplistic? Do this instead: Make half a dozen 4 x 4 checkerboards to use for later projects. Find your most comfortable ways to spread fabric and cut layers of strips. Try to improve the speed and accuracy with which you sew the strips.

If you've done lots of strip-quilt projects, and the rotary cutter is like an extension of your arm:

1. Skim over Chapter 1.

2. Skim over Chapter 2.

Steps 3, 4, and 5 are for everyone:

3. Study Chapter 3 thoroughly. Make several sizes of checkerboards and turn them on the bias.

Don't leave this section until you're comfortable with these ideas and could turn a 4 x 4 checkerboard on the bias in your sleep (or at least without looking at the pictures).

Complete some projects if you

wish. Or just make up checker-boards, turn them on the bias, and set them aside. Most projects in this book start with panels like these and you can decide later which ones to make. (It's like baking loaves of bread and putting them in the freezer to use later for any kind of sandwich you need.)

4. Look through the rest of the book.

5. Pick your next project.

Which projects should you do?

"How many projects are there in this book?"

I'm afraid someone will ask me that, and I won't know what to say. Someone once said, "You can count the seeds in an apple, but you can't count the apples in a seed." This book has a lot of projects, but even more "seeds."

There are projects. There are variations of projects. There are suggestions for projects. There are the color plates (some are other people's original projects). Then there are charts which help you plan your own projects—and an infinite number of combinations are possible there. **Page 4 lists the projects in this book.**

Notice the typography:

Bold print: These projects have yardage calculations and step-by-step instructions.

Light print: No detailed instructions are given, but you probably don't need them. These are variations of other projects, or are quite easy to calculate yourself. Most pillows are in light print: I show you how to make only the block; you add the borders and backing.

Italics: Even less information is given. These projects are for creative people who just need an idea or two and they'll take off on their own. They wouldn't do it my way if I did tell them how much yardage to use and how wide to make their borders. So I don't.

I've tried to rank projects in order of difficulty. As a rule, projects at the top of each list are plainer, those at the bottom more interesting. Don't try an advanced project without studying the ideas that lead up to it.

What makes a project "advanced"?

● Its size. With small blocks it's harder to line up seams. With large projects, the cutting strategy might be more complex and there's more sewing and quilting to do.

● The number of new ideas included.

● How easily the seams line up.

● How many squares there are and how many triangles. (Squares are easier, triangles harder but more interesting.)

Projects in this book

Bold print: Complete directions
Light print: Brief directions
Italics: Ideas for more projects

1. Some Basics

Fabric to use for blocks

Stripes, checks, plaids, or designs with dots or flowers arranged in straight or diagonal lines are not recommended for strip-quilt techniques. For one thing, you might not like the direction the design takes in the final blocks. And you can cut only one layer at a time because you have to watch the alignment of the design as you go.

To add to your troubles, the designs aren't always printed in lines that correspond with the weave of the fabric. With directional prints, you often have to choose between cutting to match the design or cutting along the grain of the fabric, because you can't do both.

Directional prints can be hard to spot, so check carefully. Some of the artwork in this book uses directional designs, but that's because of limitations in my computer graphics. Fortunately, it's different with fabric. We live at a time when there's an overwhelming selection of solid colors and random prints to choose from. Locating the perfect fabric is half the fun.

Use firmly woven fabric, 100% cotton if possible. Fast Patch specializes in triangle-based designs;

that means working on the bias a lot of the time. Sleazy, loosely woven fabric is a handicap you don't need. I especially like the homespun-type cotton solids. Their rougher texture prevents layers of fabric from sliding out of place.

In summary, when choosing fabrics for the blocks, **look for:**

- Good-quality fabric, tightly woven, 100% cotton
- Solid colors or small random prints

Avoid:

- Very large prints
- Stripes and diagonal prints
- Polyester or other synthetics

You have more leeway in choosing fabric for plain blocks, borders, and backing. If you can't resist plaids or pin dots, use them there.

Prewash or not?

Prewash fabrics to guard against possible shrinking or color bleeding. (But if you want to buy fabrics at the store where you're taking a class and use them immediately, the world won't come to an end. Use a quality brand of fabric and pale colors to be safe.)

Tools

1. A rotary cutter. This wonderful tool has a razor-sharp blade which revolves like a pizza cutter and can cut through several layers of fabric at a time, quickly and precisely. Get the large-blade type.

The blade is guarded by a cover which you push back in place after use. If you're forgetful, choose a model with a blade cover that automatically retracts like the guard on a power saw. Replace the blade when it gets dull (which might be in two or three months with normal use, immediately if you run over a pin).

2. A cutting mat. This protects the table top and keeps the blade sharp longer. Get the largest mat you can afford and have room for; I usually use a 24" x 36" size. I don't think the printed grid is necessary since you have the grid on the ruler, but I do like the new Omnimat® that reverses to a different color because it contrasts with any color of fabric.

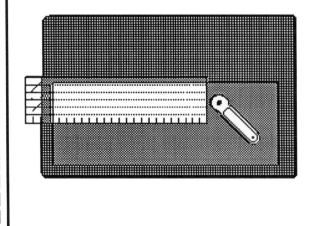

3. A 6" x 24" transparent ruler. These rulers are thick and durable with a 1" grid and a 45° angle mark. Several good brands are available. Omnigrid® rulers have yellow, as well as black, marks, which show up well on both dark and light fabrics. The 1/8" marks in both directions are essential.

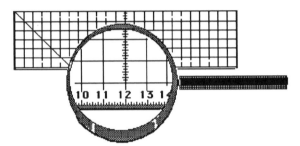

• Rulers are **transparent** so you can measure strips and cut them without drawing guidelines.

• They're **thick** so you can push against them as you cut without having the blade jump the edge.

• They're **wide** because you often use 5" or 6" strips with Fast Patch.

Tip: *Your ruler may tend to slide out of place when you cut. Spread clear nail polish on the back in several spots and sprinkle immediately with* **salt** *to make the ruler less slippery.*

Using the cutting tools

It might take a little practice to get used to the rotary cutter, but it's well worth it. Once you are skilled, you can cut through up to eight layers at a time faster than you can cut through a single layer with scissors. It's also much more accurate. Best of all, there are no guidelines to draw.

How to cut strips through several layers

Here's how to cut 4" strips, a very common strip size in this book:

1. Spread out layers of fabric with at least two edges aligned. Place the ruler over the stack 1/4" or so inside the edge.

2. Spread out one hand to hold the ruler so it doesn't slip. **Cut with the other hand,** pushing firmly against the edge of the ruler. Trim off the edges.

3. Change your position. Walk around the table or turn the mat so you can continue to cut in a natural and comfortable way. Never try to cut with the wrong hand or cross one hand over the other to cut.

4. Move the ruler over so that the edge of the fabric is at the 4" line. Cut, again pushing firmly against the ruler.

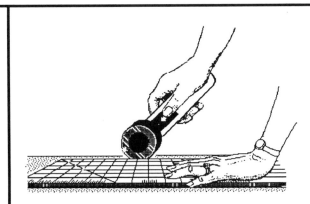

5. Cover the blade when you're done, unless you have the type with a cover that automatically pops back into place. These blades are sharp and can give you a nasty cut if you're careless.

How to use the ruler as a T-square

1. To get perfect squares for the checkerboard, etc., trim ends of panels to even them up before cutting cross sections. Then keep seams parallel to the straight lines on the ruler. You may need to trim off the end again after cutting a couple of strips to keep things squared up.

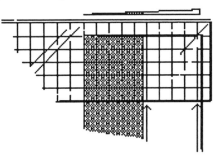

2. Take advantage of the 45° angle marks on the ruler whenever appropriate.

Sewing and pressing

1. Use thread that's a neutral color or matches your lightest fabric. A fine thread (designed for machine embroidering) is wonderful.

2. Use a size 70 (10/11) needle.

3. Sew with 1/4" seams. Most people line up the fabric with the presser foot. It's nice if your machine allows you to de-center the needle to get a seam exactly 1/4" wide. If a 5/16" seam works better for you, that's okay. The important thing is to keep all seams **exactly** the same width.

4. Use a fairly small stitch (12 stitches to the inch) and **balanced tension.** No backstitching is possible most of the time. There's usually no problem with a seam coming unstitched unless you pick out a seam that crosses it later. Avoid really tiny stitches that make it too hard to correct seams.

5 Press seams before crossing with another seam, or at least **finger-press** to keep from having tucks.

6. Press toward one side. Press **toward the darker** fabric when possible, especially if using very light fabrics. Otherwise, traces of dark fabric will show through the light areas when the project is finished. At some stages, you can't press all seams toward the dark fabric; correct that in later stages when possible.

7. Press in the direction which creates the least bulk, with the fewest seams crossing at one point. Press seams on the top layer one direction, and those on the bottom layer the other direction.

When doing projects in Chapters 3 to 8, you'll be working on the bias a lot. Here are a couple more rules for those chapters:

8. Use spray starch when pressing the checkerboard.

9. Avoid pressing bias edges. You can distort fabric easily.

Accuracy in sewing the blocks

The more accurate you are, the nicer your blocks will turn out, of course. Spot-check whenever you press. Ask yourself:

• Are all strips **cut** exactly the same width? Are **seams** even?

• Are **cross sections** cut exactly the same width as first strips?

• Are cross sections cut at **right angles to the seams?** (Did you use your ruler as a T-square as shown on page 7?)

• **Do seams line up well?**

Keeping squares square

When making a checkerboard, make sure squares are square. For projects in Chapter 2, if they **look** square, they're okay. But for projects in the rest of the book, they must **be** square or the triangles will be skewed.

To check your squares, place a ruler diagonally across the checkerboard. It should intersect the seams in an orderly manner. If it doesn't, that's a warning flag. Squares are wider one direction than the other.

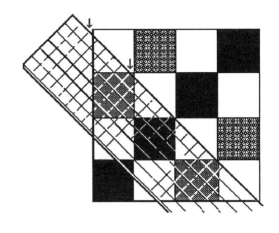

Accuracy in assembling the quilt top

1. Line up edges of blocks (and sashing, if you use it).

2. Line up seams in blocks with seams in nearby blocks. Narrow sashing needs more accuracy than wide sashing, and setting blocks next to each other requires the most accuracy of all. Alternating with plain blocks is easiest.

3. Keep blocks turned the same way when possible. Your blocks might be slightly longer in the direction of the final seams.

4. Cut plain blocks exactly the same size as the patchwork blocks. Measure several blocks to find the correct size.

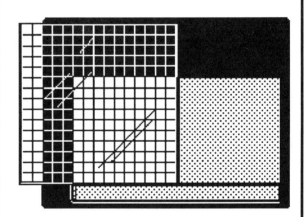

A large plastic grid like this (similar to the rulers but 12" to 15" square) is wonderful for cutting large squares quickly. Line up the grid along two edges of the fabric and trim edges. Then reposition the ruler so that it covers a square the size you want and trim the other two edges.

Designing your quilt top

This book concentrates on interesting ways to make patchwork blocks. Once you have your blocks made, how you combine them into an overall design is up to you. Directions given with the projects are just to get you started. Feel free to change the borders or anything else, especially if you've had a lot of quiltmaking experience. Have fun.

You don't always have to decide ahead of time how to assemble your blocks. The surest way is to lay out the finished blocks on the floor and to try different effects. Here are some of your options:

Alternate patchwork blocks and plain blocks.

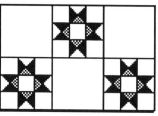

This is the quickest way to make a large quilt top. The plain blocks double the size and there are fewer seams to line up with each other. You have the opportunity (or duty, depending on your point of view) to do some quilting in the empty blocks, so plan ahead.

Alternate blocks with simple connecting blocks.

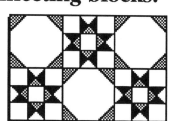

A new pattern emerges which might dramatically change the design. The diagram shows the most commonly used connecting block, which also leaves big areas to fill with quilting.

Alternate blocks with totally different blocks.

Possibilities are endless here. See Chapter 7 for some projects with small blocks. In this example the alternate block is the same block with a different color scheme. Experiment with actual blocks, sketches, or photocopies.

Set blocks adjacent to each other.

I seldom do this because the new pattern often looks like a giant plaid instead of patchwork blocks, but I do like it for the puzzle blocks in Chapter 7.

Sashing

Setting blocks with sashing

These borders between blocks frame the blocks and set them off. The number you need is shown on the chart below. You may have short and long strips, or all short strips if you have contrasting squares at the intersections. Short strips and squares may extend to the inner border around the blocks too.

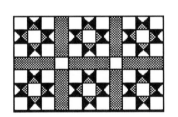

Piecing sashing and contrasting squares

1. Cut strips for the contrasting squares. Find the total number of contrasting squares needed and multiply that by the number of inches wide each square will be. Cut strips to equal that length, adding a few more inches to each strip for good measure.

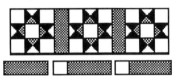

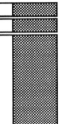

2. Cut strips for sashing. Make them as wide as the blocks and as long as the strips cut for contrasting squares.

3. Sew the strips together and cut cross sections.

4. Cut more strips without contrasting squares to equal the total shown on the chart below.

Blocks Used	Solid sashing (no contrasting squares)		Contrasting squares used		Contrasting squares in first border too	
	Short Strips	Long Strips*	Sashing	Squares	Sashing	Squares
9 (3 x 3)	6	2	12	4	24	16
12 (3 x 4)	8	3	17	6	31	20
15 (3 x 5)	10	4	22	8	38	24
16 (4 x 4)	12	3	24	9	40	25
20 (4 x 5)	15	4	31	12	49	30
24 (4 x 6)	18	5	38	15	58	35
25 (5 x 5)	20	4	40	16	60	36
30 (5 x 6)	24	5	49	20	71	42
36 (6 x 6)	30	5	60	25	84	49
42 (6 x 7)	35	6	71	30	97	56

*Doesn't include inner borders, although they usually are cut at the same time. See page 12.

Borders

Borders are like the icing on the cake, the gilded frame on the painting, the flower bed around the lawn. They almost always improve the appearance of the quilt. Experiment with different effects. (That's easiest when you have lots of fabric on hand.) Here are some ideas:

Design tips:

- **Have inner borders match sashing** or be slightly wider.

- Consider using a **sawtooth** border. See Chapter 6 for calculations and instructions.

- If borders are more than 3" wide, plan on **quilting a design** in them.

- **Binding** should be considered one of the borders. Plan its color as carefully as you do the other borders.

- It's usually more pleasing to have the **outer borders wider** than inner borders, although narrow accent borders can be used anywhere.

- **Contrasting squares in the corners** often look nice, especially if you want an Amish look.

- Consider **extending the design** into the borders.

- **Printed border fabrics** often give a truly elegant look.

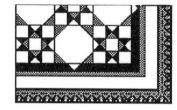

Craftsmanship tips:

- **Cut borders with the grain** if you have a choice. Fabric doesn't have as much give in that direction.

- **Avoid ruffled edges** that may result if the inner part of the quilt is bunched up from quilting but the borders aren't. You may deliberately cut the final borders a bit small and ease the quilt to fit them if you think this might be a problem.

- **Lapping borders at the corners** is much faster and is fine for everyday quilts. **Mitered borders** are almost always more attractive, especially with border prints.

- You may be able to **tear rather than cut** borders if you're making an everyday quilt from 100% cotton. Allow a wider seam if you do.

Quilting the project

To prepare for quilting:

1. Press quilt top and backing fabric.

2. Cut batting slightly larger than the quilt top and backing still larger.

3. Spread out backing wrong side up on a table, bed, or quilting frame.

4. Spread out batting over the backing, being careful not to stretch it.

5. Spread out quilt top, right side up.

6. Baste or pin thoroughly (unless it'll be quilted on a frame).

• **Hand-quilt wall hangings and masterpieces.** This is nicest because the stitching pattern complements the patchwork and adds another design element. But it's very time-consuming if the project is large.

• **Do machine quilting for speed and durability.** This can add beauty if done skillfully, but most people find doing large projects difficult. Do plenty of basting or pinning with safety pins. Plan straight lines or gentle curves; avoid lots of direction-changing. Roll project up to fit under machine.

• **Tie quilts for everyday use.** This is the fastest and easiest method, especially if you prefer thick batting, but it doesn't complement the patchwork design as much. Make knots with yarn or No. 5 pearl cotton. Between knots, yarn can go on front or back of project and be clipped and tied, or you can run the yarn though the inside so knots are not obvious.

Here is a quilt being tied. The quilt top is pinned to the backing, which has been tacked to a simple homemade frame.

Beautiful hardwood frames with many nice features can be purchased.

Note: *There are many fine books which give more details on all these techniques. See Recommended Reading, page 181.*

Binding the project

Many fine books give special attention to binding quilts. But here are some brief suggestions for one way to do it.

1. After quilting the project, spread it out on a flat surface. Use your rotary cutter to **trim the three layers** flush with each other. Slide your cutting mat along under the project as you go. The wide ruler helps you measure the outer border and keep it perfectly even as you cut. Round corners slightly.

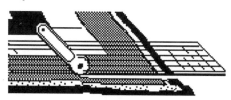

2. Measure to find the distance around the project. Cut 2-1/2" binding strips (from a more durable fabric if possible) to total that length plus 10 or 12 extra inches.

3. Turn the project over. Pin binding in place for the first edge (don't start at a corner). **Stitch through all layers** 1/2" from

edge. Stop at the corner. Fold up an extra inch of fabric and skip over it. Pin the next side. Start stitching again right next to last stitch. Continue around the quilt until you get back to the beginning. Overlap edges an inch or so and fold under final edge.

4. Bring binding around to the front and pin thoroughly. **Blind-stitch** by hand. Miter corners neatly and hand-stitch them.

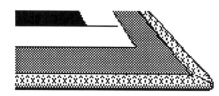

Other ideas:

1. For more durable binding, use a double layer (French binding).

2. Bring backing to front of project to form binding (or take front to back).

3. Make continuous bias binding, or buy wide bias binding.

How many yards of binding do you need? Look at the quilt sizes in the chart on page 15 and use the chart below:

Quilt Size	Binding	Quilt Size	Binding
1	6 yds.	5	11-1/2 yds.
2	9-1/2 yds.	6	12 yds.
3	10 yds.	7	12-1/2 yds.
4	10-1/2 yds.		

Backing yardage for projects in this book

Extra-wide muslin is a favorite with hand quilters. You could also use a muslin bed sheet or 60" or 90" fabric for backing, but don't use a tightly woven polyester blend if you'll be hand quilting. If you're tying or machine quilting the project, you appreciate dark prints and will probably have to use regular width fabric to get what you want. Here are some common quilt sizes, along with yardage needed for backing with 44-45" fabric. Remove the selvage; then cut and seam as shown in diagrams. (You might use the remnant to help make your quilt top.)

Type of quilt	Size (approx.)	Remnant (approx.)	Yardage
1. Twin throw	up to 54" x 72"	15" x 50"	3 yds.
2. Twin spread, double throw	up to 72"x 87"	none	4 yds.
3. Queen throw, double coverlet	76" x 90"	11" x 90"	5 yds.
4. Queen coverlet, king throw	87" x 90"	none	5 yds.
5. Waterbed, double spread	87" x 108"	none	6 yds.
6. Queen spread	99" x 108"	23" x 99"	8-1/3 yds.
7. King spread	108" sq.	23" x 108"	9 yds.

Lining and stuffing small quilts

Quick-turn method to bind edges

Use this for a baby quilt or for small everyday quilts.

1. Spread out quilt top and backing (right sides together). Trim backing to match quilt top, rounding corners slightly and clipping them. Pin edges together.

2. Trim batting to fit. Be careful not to stretch it.

3. Sew around the project, 1/2" from edge. Leave an opening for stuffing (1/4 to 1/3 of the narrow end) and openings near the corners wide enough to insert your hand.

4. Turn right side out. Straighten and press edges; your hand inside helps with this.

5. Roll up batting and stuff it in. Smooth it out carefully (hand inside).

6. Quilt or tie the project. Stitch opening by hand.

Envelope-style backing for a pillow

1. Measure pillow top. Cut two pieces as wide as the pillow top one way, about 2/3 as wide the other way. Hem one long edge of each piece.

2. Spread out layers like this and pin around edges:

Backing pieces, overlapping, right sides down

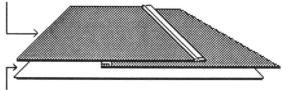

Design, right side up

3. Stitch 1/2" from the edge around entire project, backstitching to reinforce seams at the edge of each backing piece (see arrows). You may prefer to sew with the **design side** up if you have a border print around the block and want to follow the design evenly.

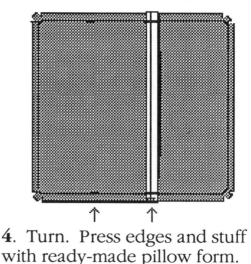

4. Turn. Press edges and stuff with ready-made pillow form.

2. Warm-up Projects

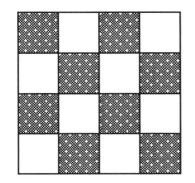

The 4 x 4 checkerboard

Most everything in this book starts as a checkerboard, often a humble "**4 x 4 checkerboard**."

Spread out light and dark fabrics, right sides together, and fold over. Cut a "stack" of strips, 4" wide and 17" long. That makes two light and two dark strips, which you sew together as shown below.

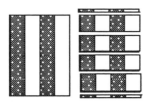

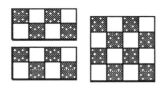

Press, trim off ends, and cut cross sections, also 4".

Reverse some strips, sew them together in pairs, and join pairs to make the panel.

Tip: *If you're not careful, you might find that the two halves won't match! It's easy to avoid that problem. Just have the **dark** fabric on top going through the machine first as you sew each pair together. You'll be making dozens of checkerboards in this book, so get in this habit.*

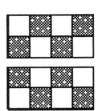

A checkerboard pillow

Is using the rotary cutter awkward for you? Make several more checkerboards. Save them to use later, or make a pillow.

Cut four 1" borders of an accent fabric, and four 3" borders of a fabric already used. Make backing as shown on page 16. Add ruffles or lace, if you wish, before sewing to backing. Stuff with an 18" pillow form.

The 4 x 8 checkerboard

 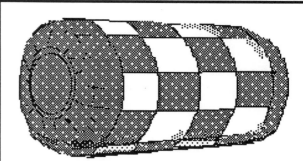

Another commonly used checkerboard in this book is the **4 x 8** size.

You could use eight short strips, but this time, use four longer ones.

Spread out light and dark fabric, right sides together, then fold over to make four layers.

Cut two stacks, 4" x 33" (eight times as long as they are wide, plus an inch to trim off). Sew strips together, cut 4" cross sections, and make them into a 4 x 8 checkerboard.

Save it for later or make a project now.

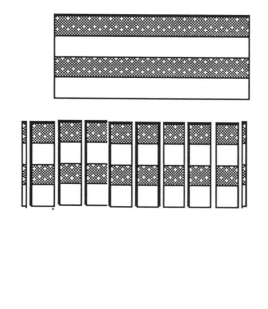

An easy neck pillow

Here's a quick gift for someone who likes to take a nap on the sofa.

1. Measure the length of the panel; it'll be about 28". Cut two borders that length and 5" wide from darker fabric.

2. Cut two circles from darker fabric about 7" across. Stay-stitch the edges.

3. Sew ends of borders together, making two cylinders. Sew gathering stitches along one edge of each. Gather the edges and sew them to the circles. (Add cording for a nice touch.)

4. Sew the two ends of the checkerboard panel to a 14" zipper, again making a cylinder. Open the zipper.

5. With right sides together, sew the border pieces to the patchwork. Stitch again to reinforce the seam.

6. Turn the pillow right side out and stuff it with polyfoam.

A checkerboard baby quilt

Make this easy project with two pastel colors (flannel, if you wish). With a 5" outer border, the size is about 38" x 52".

Fabric needed:
Dark (including backing): 2-2/3 yds.

Light: 3/4 yd.

Batting: 40" x 54"

You'll also need white yarn for tying.

1. Remove 54" from darker fabric for backing. Set it aside.

2. Remove an 11" strip for borders parallel to selvage from both fabrics.

3. Cut strips for the checkerboard. Spread out the rest of the light and dark fabric, right sides together. Fold over and cut six strips of each color, 4" x 33". Also cut three strips, 5"x 33", of **dark** to use for borders.

4. Sew strips together, alternating light and dark. Press toward dark.

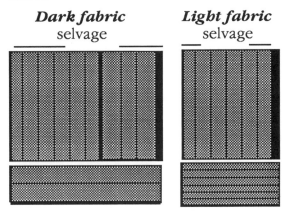

Dark fabric
selvage

Light fabric
selvage

Note: *Unless all strips are cut the same direction, I'll give cutting layouts for projects in this book. I always have the straight of the fabric horizontal.*

5. Cut cross sections. Your ruler isn't long enough to fit the width of the panel now. Try folding the panel over, wrong side out, and cutting through both layers at a time. Make sure seams on the top layer line up exactly with seams on the bottom layer. (You may find that cutting double layers isn't as accurate as you like.) Cut 4" strips.

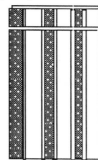

6. Sew cross sections together to make an 8 x 12 checkerboard.

7. Make borders. Cut 2" strips from the light fabric, piece, and sew in place. Add 5" borders from the darker fabric.

8. Finish quilt with the quick-turn method suggested on page 16 or any preferred method. Tie with white yarn.

Scrapbag checkerboard quilt

This cozy double bed throw, about 78" square, is very easy to make. It uses 13 checkerboards and 12 plain squares. Directions start on page 21.

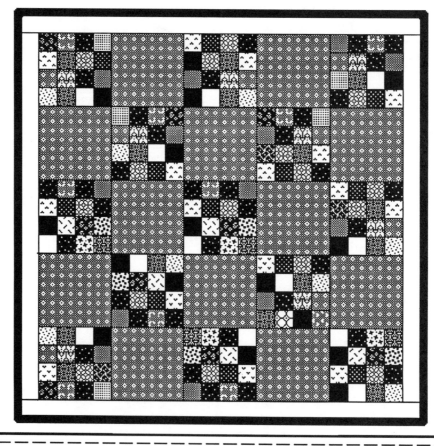

Fabric needed:

Fat quarters (18" x 22") or 1/4 yd. strips:

6 darks or dark/mediums*

6 lights or light/mediums*

Medium fabric for plain squares: 1-3/4 yds.

Muslin for border: 1 yd. (2-1/8 yds. if you don't want to piece it; use remnants for part of your light fabric for checkerboards)

Optional dark borders: 1 yd. each

Backing: 4 yds. (5 yds. if you use extra borders)

*You can use more scraps, up to 24 of dark and 24 of light, for an even prettier effect.

1. Stack fabrics, four to six layers at a time, lights and darks facing each other. Cut the equivalent of **24 light** and **24 dark** strips, 4" x 22". (If 44" strips, cut 12 light, 12 dark.)

2. Sew together in sets of four strips, alternating lights and darks.

3. Cut 4" cross sections.

4. Make 4 x 4 checkerboards, mixing up sections.

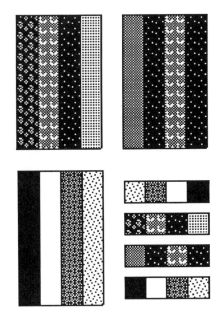

5. Cut 12 plain squares to match your checkerboards, about 14-1/2".

6. Sew plain and patchwork blocks together, making five rows of five blocks.

7. Add 4" borders from muslin and other borders if desired.

8. Make backing as shown on page 15, Number 3 or 4.

9. Tie quilt with yarn, or quilt and bind as desired.

Note: *Some of the projects in this book can be transformed to a diagonal setting, instantly setting all the blocks on point. I'll show you how on pages 39-43.*

If you want to transform this quilt: *Arrange blocks in six rows of four blocks instead. You'll have one extra block. Project will be about 68" x 87" after you turn it on the bias.*

Four-Patch quilt

This would make a colorful lap robe, about 50" square. This very old block is called a Four-Patch, because there are four squares in each block. Each block is also a 2 x 2 checkerboard.

Choose five dark fabrics, then find a nicely coordinated light/medium partner for each.

Join your finished blocks like this to create the neat diagonal lines of dark squares in the final quilt.

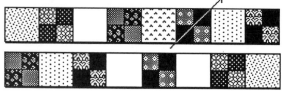

Fabric needed:

Long scraps, or 1/4 yd. pieces*: 5 dark and 5 medium

Light*: 4 or 5 long scraps at least 6" wide

Any color (borders): 1/4 yd. for narrow, 2/3 yd. for wider.

Backing: 3 yds. (You can make 54" square ahead of time as shown in Number 1, page 15. Use the 35" x 54" remnant for blocks or borders.)

Or use limited colors:
1/2 yd. dark fabric, 1/2 yd. medium fabric, and 3/4 yd. muslin

1. Cut 10 strips of fabric, 3" x 44". Arrange each pair, right sides together. Then (a) stack two or three pairs as shown, and cut long stacks, **or** (b) fold over each pair to make four layers and cut one pair at a time. (One purpose of these projects is to find your favorite ways to stack and cut strips.)

2. Sew pairs together.

3. Cut 3" sections. Sew into **32 Four-Patch blocks.** (You'll have leftovers.)

4. Make 32 large light squares. Here's how: Make a stack of four light fabrics. Cut a stack of strips as wide as the Four-Patch blocks (about 5-1/2"). Cut the stack into squares, making more from another piece if needed to make 32.

5. Join sets with plain squares, keeping darks going the direction shown on page 22. Make two types of rows, four of each, mixing up colors in a random pattern.

6. Join rows to make quilt top.

7. Cut borders in whatever fabrics and widths you prefer.

8. Make backing (page 15, Number 1). **Quilt and bind** with your favorite techniques.

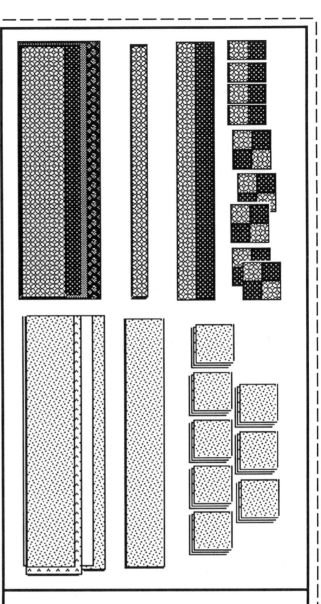

Note: *If you want to transform this project as shown on pages 39-43, you have two choices:*

1. Arrange the blocks in 10 rows of six blocks each. You'll have four leftover blocks. The project will be about 43" x 50" when turned on the bias.

2. Make a few more blocks (a total of 35 plain and 35 Four-Patch) and make 10 rows of seven blocks. The project will be about 43" x 57".

Two quilts from checkerboards and Four-Patch blocks

The small quilt shown is about 46" x 68"; use it for a twin throw or a TV quilt. Calculations for a larger quilt are on page 25.

If you put this quilt together correctly, you'll have neat chains of little dark squares going diagonally across it one direction and chains of light squares crossing the other direction.

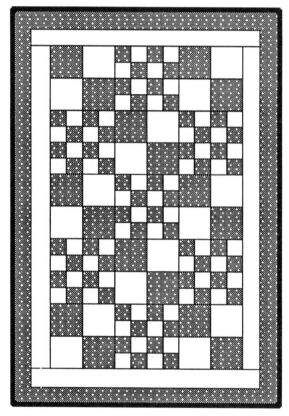

Fabric needed:

Light fabric: 1-3/4 yds.

Dark fabric: 1-3/4 yds.

Backing: 2-3/4 yds.

Batting: 48" x 72"

1. Remove fabric for borders. Remove a 16" strip along the selvage of both light and dark fabric. Set aside.

2. Cut strips. Use the cutting layout for the remaining parts of the dark and light fabric; both fabrics are cut exactly the same.

Spread out light and dark fabrics, right sides together. Fold over to make four layers if you wish.

(a) Cut **four light** and **four dark** strips, 6" x 28".

(b) Cut **eight light** and **eight dark** strips, 3-1/4" x 28".

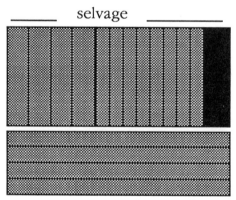

Cutting layout for both dark and light

3. Make blocks from the 6" strips: Sew strips together in pairs. Cut 6" sections. Sew together two at a time to make eight large Four-Patch blocks.

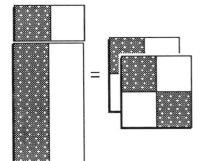

4. Make 4 x 4 checkerboards from the narrow strips. Sew four strips together and cut cross sections 3-1/4" wide. (You need only seven checkerboards, but you will have enough strips for eight. You can discard less accurate sections, or make a pillow, or use eight checkerboard blocks and only seven Four-Patch blocks.) Both types of blocks should be about 11-1/2" square.

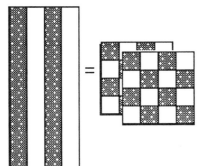

5. Sew the quilt top together. Sew blocks into rows of three blocks (three rows with one arrangement, two with the other). Keep the center seams in the blocks carefully aligned. (If some blocks are larger than others, you may need to trim the edges a bit,

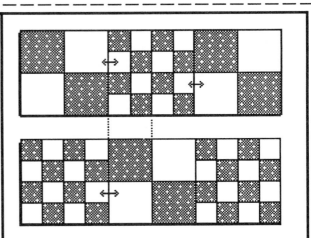

but line up that center seam first.) Be careful with the position of the lights and darks (see the arrows) to get the nice overall effect.

6. Make 4" borders from the reserved strips. Sew sides on first and then the ends, to avoid piecing.

7. Make backing, using Number 1 on page 15.

8. Quilt and bind with your favorite method.

To make a larger quilt:
Make a double bed throw or twin coverlet about 68" x 86":

1. Use 3 yds. of light and 3 yds. of dark fabric.

2. Make twice as many strips. You can use the same cutting strategy.

3. Make 30 blocks, 15 of each type, and make **six rows of five blocks** each.

4. Get 4 yds. of backing fabric; use arrangement Number 2 on page 15.

Roman Stripe baby quilt

This project is about 34" x 44". This is one of the easiest projects of all—straight strips in each block and hardly any seams to line up!

Fabric needed

Light fabric: 2/3 yd.

Dark fabric: 1-3/4 yds. (includes backing)

Batting: 36" x 46"

1. Cut strips. Stack and fold so you can cut twice as many dark strips as light ones. One way: Spread the light fabric over the dark, lining up two edges, then fold over another layer of dark to make three layers. Cut five stacks (five strips of light and ten of dark) 2-1/4" wide and 44" long. Then cut two 4" stacks for borders. (The

light borders will be divided later into 2" borders.)

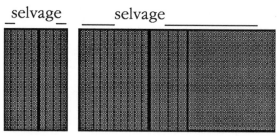

Light fabric   *Dark fabric*

2. Sew strips together. Make sets of three strips and press toward the dark.

3. Cut blocks. Measure the width of these three-strip sets, using the edge of the ruler (it'll be about 5-3/4"). Then cut cross sections that same size and you will have 35 blocks all made.

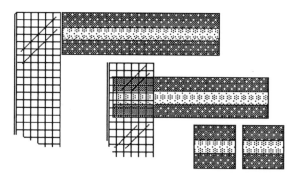

4. Sew blocks together, turning blocks so you alternate between vertical stripes and horizontal stripes. If blocks don't line up perfectly, just trim some a bit. (Don't try that with most blocks!)

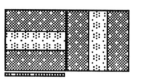

(overleaf) Projects from Chapter 8: green quilt by Sue Pepper of Springfield, OR, from 9″ blocks of Sister's Choice D, machine quilted; pillows by Anita Hallock using Crown of Thorns (page 145) and Fool's Square/Pinwheel blocks (page 147).

(above) This visual aid for teaching Fast Patch was made by Ruby Sharman of Reedsport, OR. The block demonstrated is Sister's Choice C, the most popular block in Chapter 8.

(below) Projects pieced and machine-quilted by Anita Hallock: Three-Patch sampler based on page 120 with slight changes; Five-Patch Pinwheel wall hanging, an advanced project, from page 154; Ohio Star using Variation F blocks (page 88) and 3″ Alpha strips.

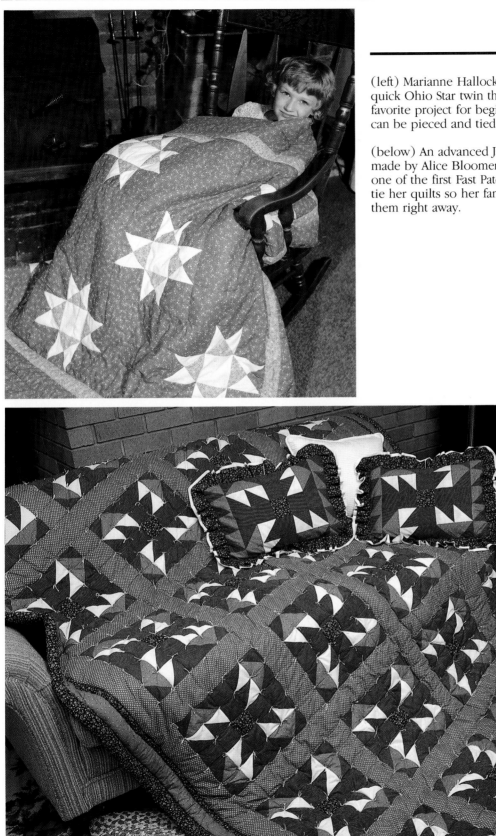

(left) Marianne Hallock wrapped in Anita's quick Ohio Star twin throw (page 82), a favorite project for beginners because it can be pieced and tied in the same day.

(below) An advanced Jack-in-the-Box quilt made by Alice Bloomer of Springfield, OR, one of the first Fast Patchers. Alice likes to tie her quilts so her family can enjoy using them right away.

(right) Elaine Royster of Mt. Airy, NC, used cheerful bandana prints for this Ohio Star quilt. She used 20 large blocks of 4″ Alpha strips (Variation C, page 87). It was made quickly and tied so she won't need to fret if her grandson takes it camping.

(below) The project on the ironing board is a simple Rail Fence baby quilt, turned on the bias (page 44), made by Ruth Ohlen of Sewing Plus in Corvallis, OR. Hanging from the towel rack is a Two-Color Ohio Star with a third color in the center, made by Betsey Marshall of Niantic, CT. The stove is owned by Dorsy Hancock.

Make three rows like this:

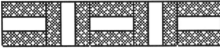

Make four like this:

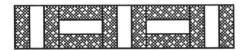

5. Join rows. Seams must line up from row to row, but again, it's easy to cheat a little. Just widen a seam here and there, or even taper them.

6. Add borders. (Divide the 4" **light** strips into four 2" borders.)

7. Quilt and bind project with your favorite method.

Rail Fence quilts

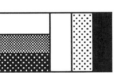

The baby quilt is as easy to sew as a Roman Stripe, but directions are a little more complicated because there are five colors and two slightly different blocks which must be combined in a certain pattern to get the right effect.

For a baby quilt or lap robe:

Make 56 blocks, 5-1/4" square. Finished size is about 40" x 56".

Fabric needed:

Light: 1 yd.

Medium A and Dark A: 1/3 yd. each

Medium B and Dark B: 2/3 yd. each

Backing: 1-1/2 yds.

Batting: 42" x 58"

1. Cut strips. Here's how:

(a) Spread out Dark A, Medium A, and the light fabric with two edges even. Fold over to make six layers. Cut **four stacks** (12 strips, folded) 2-1/4" x 44".

(b) Stack Dark B and Medium B with the light fabric as before. Cut **nine stacks**, 2-1/4" x 44". Four stacks (12 strips) are for the blocks; the rest will be used for the borders.

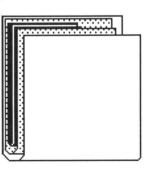

2. Sew the strips to each other in sets like this: light, then medium, then dark. Make eight sets, four of each type.

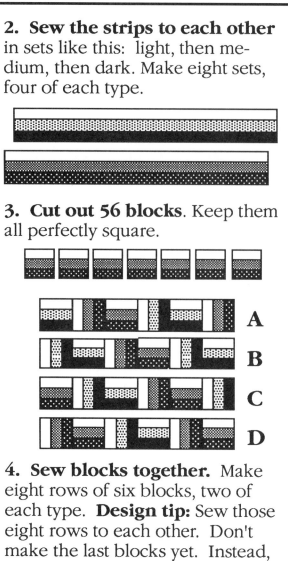

3. Cut out 56 blocks. Keep them all perfectly square.

A
B
C
D

4. Sew blocks together. Make eight rows of six blocks, two of each type. **Design tip:** Sew those eight rows to each other. Don't make the last blocks yet. Instead, spread them out next to the finished quilt top and see which end needs more blocks to balance colors, etc. Also see pages 42-45. If you want to turn this quilt on the bias, don't add the ninth row because you need an even number of rows for that step.

5. Cut borders. Use the five extra stacks of strips cut in Step 1, piecing as needed. You can change the order of the borders if you want.

6. Quilt and bind with your favorite method.

For a twin quilt, about 67" x 90", use 7-1/2" blocks.

Fabric needed:

Light fabric: 2 yds.

Medium A and Dark A: 2/3 yds. of each

Medium B and Dark B: 1-1/4 yds. of each

Backing: Measure project (will be 4 or 5 yds.)

Batting: 70" x 92"

1. Follow the same cutting strategy. Cut seven stacks of each fabric layout, plus seven extra stacks for the borders. Make all strips 3" x 44".

2. Make 14 sets of three strips each, seven of each type.

3. Cut 70 blocks. Make 10 rows of seven blocks each.

4. Make borders and backing (page 15, Number 2 or 3).

5. Quilt and bind with your favorite method.

Note: *This quilt can be turned on the bias with no special adjustment. See pages 42-45. Size will be about the same after turning.*

Nine-Patch baby quilt (Irish Chain arrangement)

Nine-Patch blocks are among the oldest and most common blocks. When set like this, the squares create diagonal "chains," so it's called Irish Chain. This 34" x 44" project has 18 blocks alternating with 17 squares.

Fabric needed:

Light fabric: 1 yd.

Dark fabric: 2 yds. (includes backing)

Batting: 36" x 46"

1. Cut strips. Lay out light and dark fabric, right sides together. Fold over to make four layers and cut five strips of each color, 2-1/4" x 44".

Light Fabric	*Dark Fabric*
__selvage___	_____selvage_____

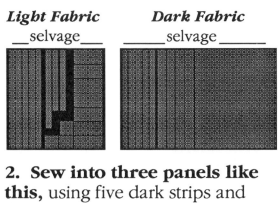

2. Sew into three panels like this, using five dark strips and four light strips. (Set one light strip aside for borders.)

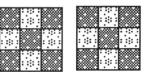

3. Cut cross sections 2-1/4" wide.

4. Assemble 18 blocks. (You'll have one or two extra cross sections of each type; discard the less accurate ones.)

5. Cut 17 squares to match blocks (about 5-3/4" square) from the **light fabric.** (Follow the cutting layout; you need a long piece left over for borders.)

6. Assemble the blocks and plain squares to make quilt top.

7. Add borders. Use reserved light strip and cut three more 2-1/4" borders from light fabric. Use four strips 4" x 44" from dark fabric. Sew side borders on first, then top and bottom borders.

8. Complete the project, turning as shown on page 16. Tie with white yarn.

Note: *If you want to switch to a diagonal setting (page 42), you have two choices:*

1. Leave off one row of blocks. (The quilt will be narrow, about 32" x 48", depending on borders.)

2. Make two more Nine-Patch blocks and three more plain blocks and add one row. (The quilt will be wider, about 40" x 48", depending on borders.)

Nine-Patch double-bed throw

This scrapbag quilt is designed to use "fat quarters" (pieces 18" x 22"). Size is about 66" x 80".

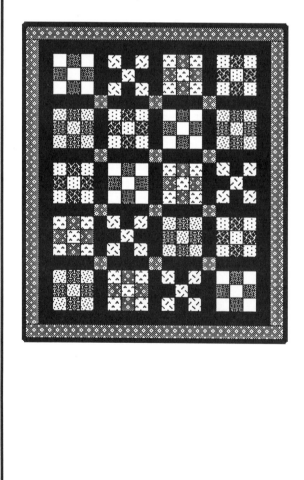

Fabric needed:

Medium fabric: 1-1/4 yds.

Dark fabric: 2 yds.

Fat quarters: 5 light fabrics, 4 dark/medium fabrics

Backing: 4 yds.

Batting: 70" x 84"

1. Cut strips. The cutting layout on page 31 applies mostly to the plain blocks and borders. You do need to **remove one piece** the size of the fat quarters (18" x 22") from the dark fabric to use for this step. (Follow the cutting layout so you don't cut up fabric needed for borders.) Arrange it and the other light and dark pieces, right sides together, using fabrics that look pretty together. Cut each arrangement into **five** stacks of strips **4" x 18"**.

2. Sew the strips in each set into panels for Nine-Patch blocks (page 29). Use **five light** and **four dark** each time. There'll be some leftover dark strips.

3. Make 20 blocks, four from each set of fabrics.

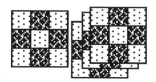

4. Make sashing with contrasting squares as mentioned on page 11. Sashing will be 4" wide, and you need 12 squares of **medium** fabric, so you need 48", plus several extra inches. Fabric is only 44" wide, so cut one strip 4" x 44" and another strip 4" x 9". Cut two strips of **dark** fabric as wide as the blocks and as long as the fabric allows (about 11" x 54"). Sew the medium strips to one of them. Cut both into 4" strips. You should

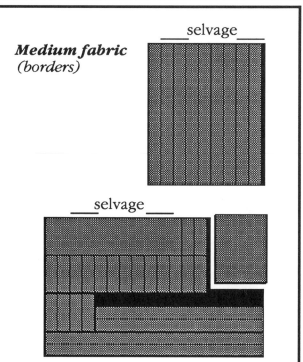

Medium fabric *(borders)*

selvage

selvage

Dark fabric

have all 12 pieces with the squares attached. You need a total of 19 strips without squares. Cut them as shown in the cutting layout.

5. Sew blocks and sashing together.

6. Add borders. Cut 4" borders lengthwise from dark fabric. Sew top and bottom borders on, then sides. Divide medium fabric into eight more 4" strips.

7. Make backing. (Use Number 2 on page 15.)

8. Quilt and bind with your favorite methods. Tie with white yarn if you wish.

Designing your own projects with Nine-Patch blocks

Chart 1 • Use this chart when making Nine-Patch blocks from 44" strips:

Size of Blocks	Width of Strips	Number of Strips Needed		Number of Blocks
		Dominant Color	Second Color	
5-1/4"	2-1/4"	5	4	18
		10	8	36
7-1/2"	3"	5	4	14
		10	8	28
9"	3-1/2"	5	4	12
		10	8	24
		15	12	36

Chart 2 • Don't use this chart until you get to Chapter 7 and start using "Beta strips." Use this when combining Nine-Patch with blocks in Chapter 7.

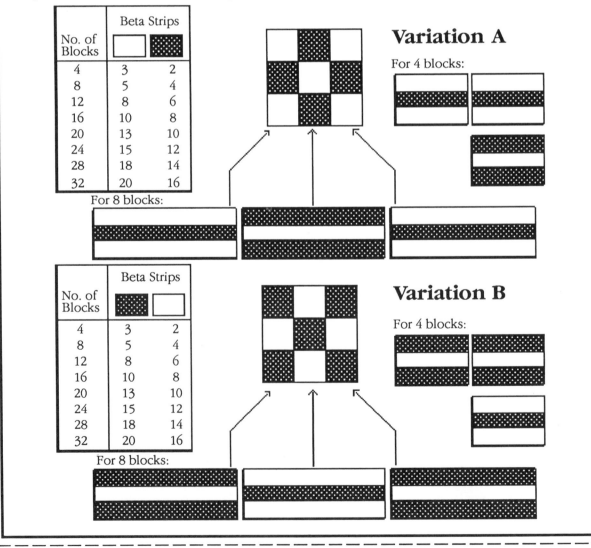

No. of Blocks	Beta Strips	
4	3	2
8	5	4
12	8	6
16	10	8
20	13	10
24	15	12
28	18	14
32	20	16

Variation A

For 4 blocks:

For 8 blocks:

No. of Blocks	Beta Strips	
4	3	2
8	5	4
12	8	6
16	10	8
20	13	10
24	15	12
28	18	14
32	20	16

Variation B

For 4 blocks:

For 8 blocks:

3. A New Direction

Working magic with diagonal cuts

By now you know you can make lots of cozy quilts without templates and tiny pieces. You do it with **strips.** Projects you make are often variations of checkerboards, which use **vertical strips** and **horizontal strips**. That's as far as most folks go; there doesn't seem to be any other direction to cut strips.

Actually, there are two more directions you can cut.

You can cut **diagonally** and make strips like this:

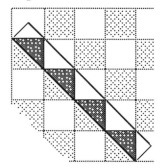

Then you can sew these strips together and cut diagonally the **other** direction and **have chains of triangles** already made!

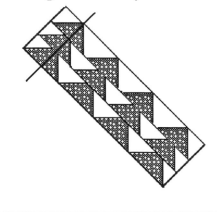

I know what you're thinking: "Wait a minute. If you cut diagonally, you make lots of funny-looking odds and ends, not real strips."

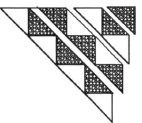

But there's an easy way around that problem, with a magical Fast Patch step.

Turn the checkerboard on the **bias:**

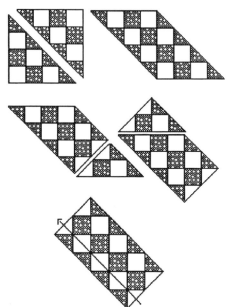

It's a surprising step, but it's not hard at all. Make two cuts and sew two seams. Then you can cut strips of triangles—long, uniform strips, squared off on the end.

You guessed it. In this chapter you'll practice turning a checkerboard on the bias.

How to turn a 2 x 4 checkerboard on the bias

First try a very small checkerboard, one with two squares one way and four squares the other. Use one light and one dark strip, 4" x 17".

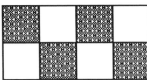

There are always four steps:

1. Cut diagonally from one corner. (It usually doesn't matter which corner.) Where the circle is, you will actually cut into the adjoining square a bit because of how the seam allowances work.

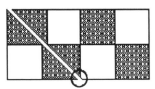

2. Move one piece over and sew it to the other side. Squares will continue the light/dark pattern, so you know that's the right spot. Again, don't worry about the circled spot. The triangle won't seem to fit the square because of the seam allowance, but it's okay.

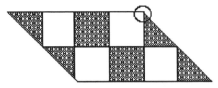

3. Cut diagonally again. Start your cut where the direction changes (at the point of the triangle).

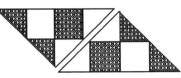

4. Sew the two pieces together again. You always sew dark squares to light squares.

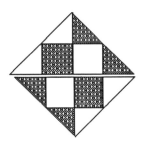

Wasn't that easy? Study it a little. You started out with a rectangle-shaped checkerboard, and now it's square. It's a collection of triangles and diamonds, not squares. You've sort of turned it inside out. You used the seam allowances that were on the outside of the checkerboard, and the triangles that used to be on the inside of the checkerboard are now on the edges.

Paper practice

Look at page 177. You can make photocopies of that big checkerboard and cut out checkerboards of different sizes. Do the practice exercises in this chapter with scissors and removable clear tape, before you try them with fabric, if you wish.

An Ohio Star block

What can you do with a little bitty checkerboard turned on the bias? Make it into an Ohio Star block.

1. Cut it into four parts, exactly through the intersections. You may want to clip the corners. Measure the sets. They'll be 4-1/2" to 5" square if you used 4" strips.

2. Cut four dark squares and **one light square** exactly that size.

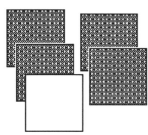

3. Sew the four dark squares to two sets of triangles (to the light triangles).

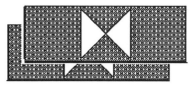

4. Sew the light square between the other two sets of triangles (to the dark triangles).

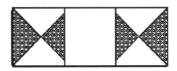

5. Assemble the block. Add borders and make it into a pillow, if you wish.

You could make several of these blocks, each from black and a different solid color. Combine them into one project.

Tip: *The tricky part of making Ohio Star is lining up the points of the triangles precisely. Try inserting a pin vertically through the points of both layers, then pinning on each side. Remove the vertical pin and sew.*

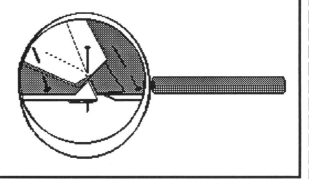

How to turn a 4 x 4 checkerboard on the bias

The 4 x 4 checkerboard is probably used more than any other size in this book. Here's how to turn it on the bias. Again, it takes four steps.

1. Cut diagonally from one corner.

2. Move one piece over and sew it to the other side. (Remember, the triangle won't match the square at the circled points.)

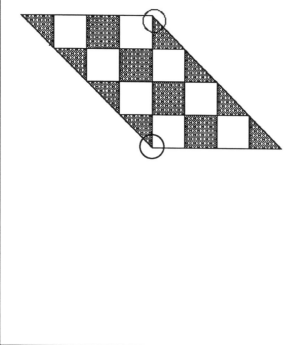

3. Cut diagonally again where the direction changes.

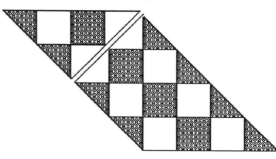

4. Sew the pieces together.

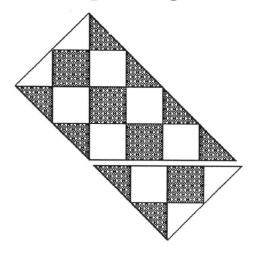

Follow this pattern for other **square** checkerboards, **6 x 6, 8 x 8, 10 x 10, 12 x 12,** etc. They always end up as **long rectangles.**

(Don't try to use checkerboards with **odd** numbers like 5 x 5 and 7 x 7. They don't work. You have to make checkerboards with the same number of dark strips and light strips, so it'll be an even number at least one direction.)

The Checker-Star wall hanging

You may want to cut the 4 x 4 bias panel into sets of triangles and make a cheerful two-star wall hanging, maybe in Christmas colors. If you used 4" strips to make the checkerboard, follow these directions. (Size will be about 18" x 32".)

1. Cut sets of triangles. Measure them.

2. Cut two squares of light fabric that size (about 4-3/4" or 5").

3. Make eight Four-Patch blocks, as shown on page 23. Cut two 2-3/4" x 44" strips, one of the dark or medium fabric already used and one of a new fabric. Sew them together. Cut 2-3/4" sections and make eight blocks.

4. Piece together triangle sets, plain squares, and Four-Patch sets to make two stars as shown.

5. Make sashing with contrasting squares. Use the technique shown on page 11. Cut a piece of fabric (the darker color in the checkerboard) as wide as the blocks (about 14") and 21" long. Sew on a strip of dark fabric 2-3/4" wide and 18" long to make the contrasting squares. Cut cross sections, making six strips with squares attached and one without. Piece together.

6. Add backing. Quilt and bind your favorite way.

Fabric needed:

Light (for checkerboard and 2 squares): 1/4 yd.

Medium or dark (includes fabric used for the original checkerboard): 2/3 yd.

Third fabric (dark in this example): 1/4 yd.

Backing: 1/2 yd.

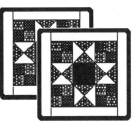

Use your imagination! Directions are just to get you started. Add a fourth color for centers or borders, make two pillows instead of one wall hanging, turn the Four-Patch blocks the other direction, etc.

How to turn a 4 x 8 checkerboard on the bias

This works like the 2 x 4 size.

1. Cut diagonally from one corner.

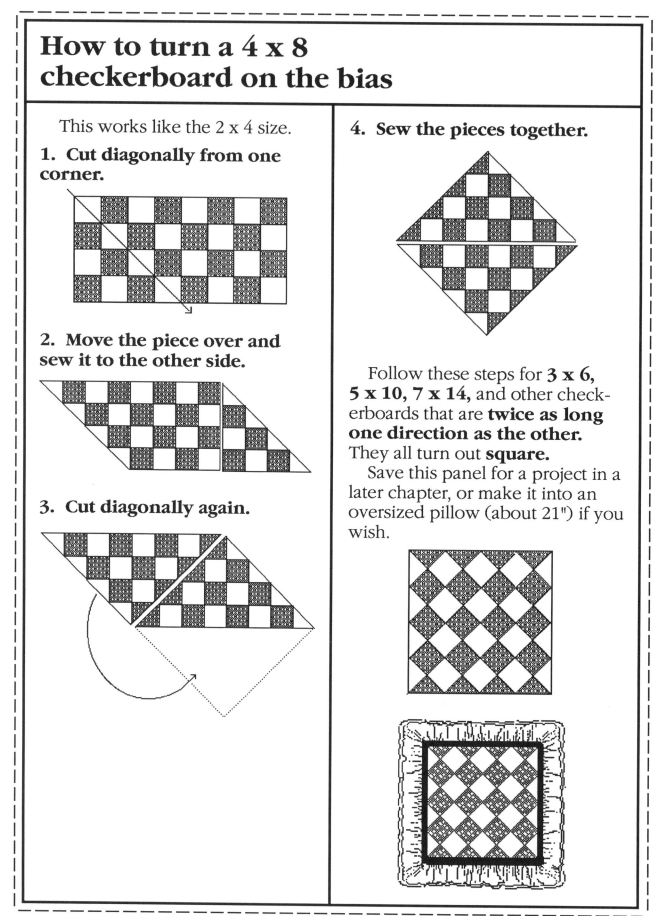

2. Move the piece over and sew it to the other side.

3. Cut diagonally again.

4. Sew the pieces together.

Follow these steps for **3 x 6, 5 x 10, 7 x 14,** and other checkerboards that are **twice as long one direction as the other.** They all turn out **square.**

Save this panel for a project in a later chapter, or make it into an oversized pillow (about 21") if you wish.

Other sizes of checkerboards

The checkerboards I have shown you so far are the most commonly used ones for the blocks in this book, but other sizes will work too.

Q. What's the smallest size of checkerboard that can be turned on the bias?

A. What's the smallest you can make? The little Four-Patch block (a 2 x 2 checkerboard) could be turned on the bias if you needed just a few triangles.

Q. What's the largest size of checkerboard that can be turned on the bias?

A. What's the largest you can make? You could turn a whole quilt top on the bias. (That's an exciting idea we'll explore on pages 40-45.) When making blocks, there is no advantage to making checkerboards larger than 8 x 8.

Q. What other sizes will work?

A. For blocks and especially for sawtooth borders, 4 x 6 or 6 x 8 checkerboards are sometimes handy. I call them "fat rectangles." Several other sizes work, but the only time you would need them would be when you were turning a whole quilt top on the bias.

On page 176 I'll show many sizes of checkerboards turned on the bias.

Q. How do you know whether an odd size checkerboard will work?

A. Make copies of page 177 and cut out the size you want to experiment with.

Follow the same steps as before. **If you're making blocks**, it's easiest to make the cut in Step 3 **where the direction changes**. (There'll be two places to choose from, marked by arrows.) This gives you dark along one edge and light on the other edge of the bias panel.

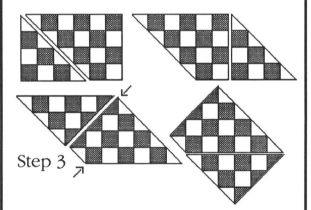

If you're turning a whole quilt top on the bias, it's different. You usually want the same fabric on all edges, so you cut through the same color you cut in Step 1. You'll need to cut somewhere **between** those two places. More about this on pages 40-45.

Turning the checkerboard baby quilt on the bias

If you started the baby quilt project on page 19, but haven't yet put borders on it, you can turn it on the bias. The final project turns out almost the same size (just a bit shorter and wider), so you can use the same yardage for borders and backing.

Craftsmanship tips:

1. Draw the cutting lines first. Then **stay-stitch** on each side of the line before cutting.

2. If your cutting mat isn't large enough, slide it along under your work as you cut.

Notice that the tips of the diamonds around the edges are lost in the seams. We'll assume that it won't bother the baby. If it bothers *you*, you can trim off most of the outer rows, leaving a 1/2" seam allowance at the tip of each diamond.

The drawing shows the tufts of yarn on the inside of each diamond. Which effect do you like better?

Cut through whichever color you want on the edges of the quilt. Make your second cut through that same color.

It's easier to get mixed up when turning fat rectangles on the bias. In the illustrations I put a big dot on one corner so you can see where that corner ends up. You could put a sticker or something on your project in that same position, if it helps.

As mentioned on page 42, use this same pattern with other fat rectangle checkerboards. It's the best width/length ratio for an overall quilt turned on the bias because your final project turns out to be about the same size as the original.

Turning quilt tops on the bias

Ignore pages 42 to 45 if you wish. These ideas are optional. Turning checkerboards on the bias is the heart of the Fast Patch system, but turning the whole quilt top on the bias was a new idea I was still exploring while writing this book.

Note: *Several projects in the book can be turned on the bias. I will tell you how to adjust the project so that step will work.*

Some general rules:

1. The quilt should have **blocks which look good on the diagonal.** Some blocks look better diagonally (Pine Trees and Baskets) and some don't look as pretty (Shoofly and Ohio Star—but that's just my opinion).

2. The overall quilt top must be a checkerboard, so use **alternating-block** arrangments. Think of the patchwork blocks as dark squares and the plain blocks as the light squares, or vice-versa.

3. You must have an even number of blocks on the longer side; you can have either even or odd blocks on the shorter side. Alternating-block quilts usually have an odd number of blocks both ways, since that puts the same block in all corners for a nicely balanced arrangement.

You'll have to change the arrangement (add a row, leave off a row, etc).

4. Cut through only the plain blocks when turning the top on the bias. First, try a paper checkerboard (from page 177) with the number of squares you have in mind. You'll find a slight irregularity sometimes, somewhat like the one shown on page 79. You can easily correct it, if you don't panic.

5. You'll lose the points of the blocks on the edge of the quilt. Pick a block with plain corners. Using the corner fabric for the borders might also help.

6. Be prepared for a change in the size and proportions of the quilt. The charts on page 176 will help you predict the size. Here's what happens to the proportions:

Original Shape	Shape When Turned on Bias
Square Long rectangle Fat rectangle	Long rectangle Square Fat rectangle*

*but not exactly the same dimensions

7. Mark your cutting line and stay-stitch, 1/4" from the line on both sides, before cutting. This will put stay-stitching around the whole outer edge of the quilt top after it as been turned on the bias, and this keeps edges from stretching.

Some projects that can be turned on the bias

Above: *Four-Patch quilt from page 22 (started as ten rows of six blocks).*

Below: *Irish Chain from page 29. The quilt started as eight rows of five blocks each. (The other alternative given was to have ten rows of five blocks each; that would have made a square quilt.)*

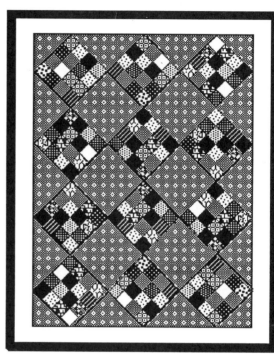

Above: *Checkerboard quilt from page 20 (started as six rows of four blocks).*

Right: *A scrapbag version of the Irish Chain would have a real old-time look. This shows 54 plain blocks and 54 Nine-Patch blocks. The original layout would be 12 rows of nine blocks each. (To make the blocks, you could use 14 combinations, four of each, or seven combinations, eight of each.)*

The Rail Fence turned on the bias

When it comes to creative things, it seems that as soon as someone makes a rule, someone breaks it with striking results. Rule 1 on page 42 was to cut only through plain blocks when turning something on the bias. That's still a good rule, but you may find exceptions, as we did with Rail Fence. Turning it on the bias made a dramatic change. See Color Plate 7. No one would believe that quilt was so simple to make.

Look at the original quilt on page 27. Those blocks alternated between vertical lines and horizontal lines. You don't think of that quilt as **checkerboard** because your eye is drawn to the "rail fence" zigzagging across the quilt.

An advantage when turning this one on the bias is that you don't notice the corners being lost in the border seams. (The corners weren't obvious to **start** with.) That might also be a disadvantage. You can't cut through the corners of the squares if you can't find them! Look closely, draw your lines, and make stay-stitching. Then cut.

On page 28 are specifications for a large Rail Fence quilt. That one can be transformed this same way—if you have a large floor to spread it out on and a lot of courage. It's not easy to cut up a quilt that's almost finished.

Design tip: *Your zigzag "fences" look better going **across** the quilt than up and down, so be careful. The **first** cut becomes the **long** edge of the quilt, and the second cut makes the **shorter** edge. Make your first cut **cross** the fence, so the second cut can go parallel to it.*

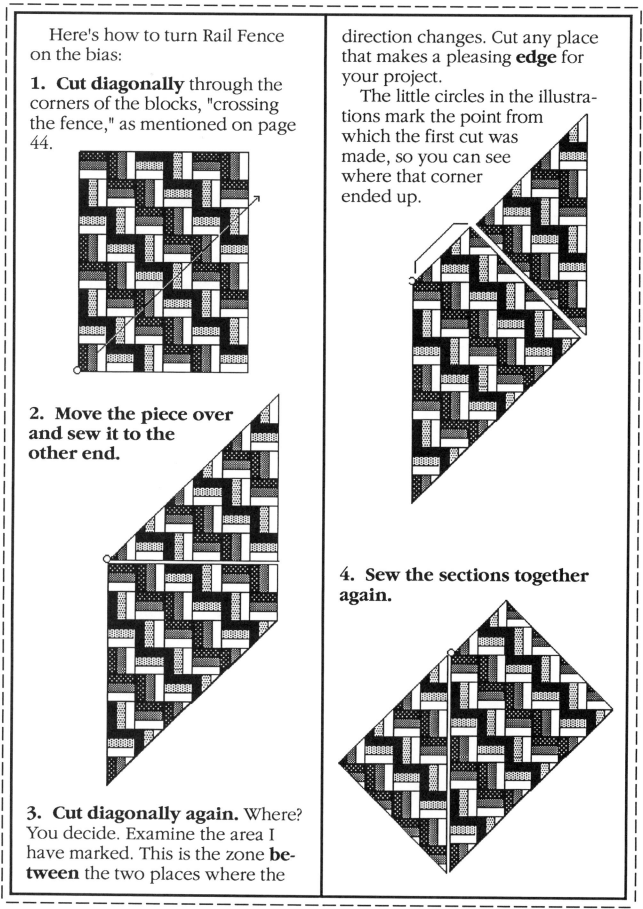

Here's how to turn Rail Fence on the bias:

1. Cut diagonally through the corners of the blocks, "crossing the fence," as mentioned on page 44.

2. Move the piece over and sew it to the other end.

3. Cut diagonally again. Where? You decide. Examine the area I have marked. This is the zone **between** the two places where the

direction changes. Cut any place that makes a pleasing **edge** for your project.

The little circles in the illustrations mark the point from which the first cut was made, so you can see where that corner ended up.

4. Sew the sections together again.

A summary of Chapter 3

The idea of turning a checker-board on the bias is an exciting one that you're just getting a taste of. I've shown you two magical things that can happen:

1. You can cut out **ready-made sets of triangles** (pages 35 and 37).

2. You can **instantly transform a pillow top or quilt top** to a diagonal arrangement (pages 38-45).

The rest of the book deals with the third magic idea:

3. You can cut **strips of triangles** with no waste, then sew them to strips which make the **squares.** There are hundreds of blocks that can be made that way.

I've shown you how to turn several sizes of checkerboard on the bias. You don't need to worry about most sizes. These two sizes are the most important:

● **The 4 x 4 checkerboard.** You could make almost any project in the book with **4 x 4** checker-boards. It's the old stand-by.

● **The 4 x 8 checkerboard.** If you're making lots of blocks,

you'll probably prefer making this size.

You may occasionally use **2 x 4** if you need just a few triangles, **8 x 8** if you're making Ohio Star (I'll show you that on page 77), **4 x 6** or **6 x 8** if you're making sawtooth chains, and odd sizes if you're turning a quilt top on the bias. Copy the checkerboard on page 177 to try odd sizes with scissors and Scotch tape.

Please don't go on to the rest of the book unless...

1. Using the rotary cutter feels natural to you, and you are comfortable spreading out layers of fabric and cutting stacks of strips.

2. Checkerboards are easy for you to make, and your seams line up quite well.

3. You understand how to turn 4 x 4 and 4 x 8 checkerboards on the bias.

4. You know some basic techniques for quilting and binding.

Keep doing projects in Chapters 2 and 3, referring to Chapter 1 for craftsmanship suggestions if necessary, until you are ready to go on. There are a lot of new ideas ahead.

Some New Ideas

The best introduction to the new ideas you'll use in the rest of the book is this chart. It shows how a set of four Ohio Star blocks is made with an interesting sequence of panels and strips. So far you've tried Steps 1 through 6. Now we'll go on through Step 11.

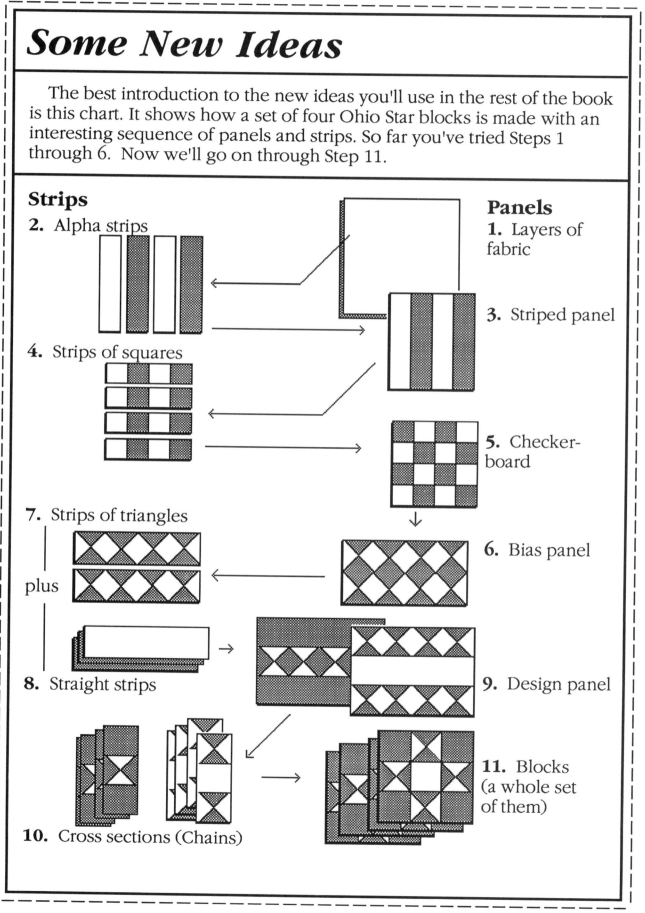

Strips

2. Alpha strips

4. Strips of squares

7. Strips of triangles

plus

8. Straight strips

10. Cross sections (Chains)

Panels

1. Layers of fabric

3. Striped panel

5. Checker-board

6. Bias panel

9. Design panel

11. Blocks (a whole set of them)

Some new terms

In the projects in Chapter 2, you usually cut strips which became simple squares. There were no firm rules about what lengths and widths were used. I just chose widths that gave the size squares you needed and lengths that were easiest to cut and fit the fabric with the least waste. From now on, however, we have some restrictions about what proportions we'll use, so I'm going to call the strips by some different names.

Alpha strips

There are usually two or three main cutting sessions in the projects I'll give you. Alpha strips are the ones cut during the first cutting session (Alpha means "first"). They are the strips which are made into **checkerboards**, which then make the **triangles** in the final blocks.

Alpha strips are normally **four times as long as they are wide, plus an inch.** The inch allows for trimming after the first panel is sewn. If you're making Ohio Star blocks, the most common sizes of Alpha strips are 3" x 13" and 4" x 17". If you're making other blocks, the most common sizes are 4" x 17" and 5" x 21".

Double-length Alpha strips are **eight times as long as they are wide, plus an inch.**

Bias panels

When checkerboards have been turned on the bias, I call them bias panels.

Strips of triangles (bias strips)

These are the strips cut from the bias panels. There is a standard size used in this book, consisting of four triangles of one color, and three and two half-triangles of the other color.

In Ohio Star blocks these strips are **double-wide**.

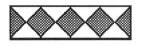

Straight strips

Straight strips make the **squares** in the final blocks. Their size varies a bit from one individual to another because some people use wider seams than others. Make them exactly the same size as the **strips of triangles**. With Ohio Star they are **four times as long as they are wide**.

Tip: *For most blocks I call straight strips "Beta Strips," but not when doing Ohio Star. The strips for Ohio Star are not typical Beta width.*

Design panels

When you have a checkerboard turned on the bias, it's an all-purpose panel which can be used for a lot of things. (That's why I said in Chapters 2 and 3 that you could save them for later.)

But when strips of triangles and straight strips are sewn together in special combinations to make one particular design, they are called **Design panels.** Diagrams like these show you what types of design panels you need to make each block.

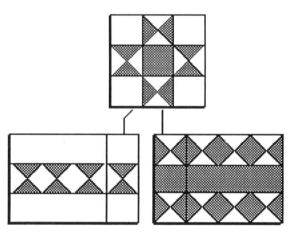

Important:

You lose points in the seams when sewing design panels, but that's okay. The **blunt points** create your seam allowance for the final chains.

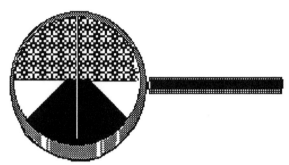

Chains

Chains are the **cross sections**, or **final strips**, of squares and triangles ready to be assembled into the blocks. Chains may be just two or three squares or triangles, or they may be several feet long if you're making a sawtooth border.

Some new rules

Look at the diagram on page 47 again. At several stages, there are some special things you can do to keep final blocks accurate.

Stage 5. Checkerboard stage:

(a) It's more important now to **have squares perfectly square**. Look at the diagram on page 9 again for a way to check them.

(b) Use **spray starch** when pressing the checkerboard to give it extra body for turning on the bias.

Stage 7. Triangle strips:

(a) Cut them on a flat surface with a rotary cutter. Don't press them or handle them too much. If they've been stretched, let them ease back into shape overnight.

(b) There will be masses of seams at some points. Clip them off. The bumps can cause your machine to balk or sew crooked, and they would detract from the finished quilt if you left them there.

Stage 8. Straight strips:

(a) Measure your triangle strips and match them exactly. Don't add a little for good measure here as you did for the Alpha strips. If your strips are slightly different sizes, use the ideal measurement (length four times the width for Ohio Star).

(b) Mark them off in four equal sections. For just a few blocks, fold each strip into fourths and notch corners. For many blocks, stack and measure sections. Mark with an Xacto knife.

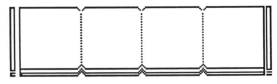

Stage 9. Design panels:

(a) Match the points of triangles to marks on the straight strips.

(b) Line up triangles on one side of the panel evenly with the ones on the other side so a straight cut goes right through all the points.

(c) Keep the blunt points evenly blunt (about 5/8").

Stage 10. Cross sections (chains): Use the markings on the ruler (including the 45° angle mark) to cut them precisely.

Stage 11. Final blocks: Choose chains which have seams most perfectly aligned for each block. Don't stretch or ease bias edges to make the seams fit. Most people have to pick out seams and adjust them occasionally, just as they would with traditional patchwork.

For all stages, use a serger if you have one. Bias edges feed into the machine more evenly with less marking and pinning.

4. *The Two-Color Ohio Star*

The Ohio Star is one of America's all-time favorite quilt blocks. It's a graceful but simple block, a pretty block in almost any fabrics. It has been the most popular block to make with Fast Patch so far, as you'll see in the color section.

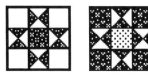

I'm spending two chapters on the Ohio Star. In Chapter 4, I do a two-color star. (It actually has three colors if you use a new color for the centers.) There are two variations, dark star on a light background and light star on a dark background. They come from identical checkerboards.

In Chapter 5 is the traditional three-color star. It might seem strange to put it in a separate chapter, but there's a good reason. The third color is worked into the checkerboard right from the start, and there are special instructions for that.

Each Ohio Star block has 16 triangles, which Grandma would have cut out one at a time and pieced together two at a time; we'll make them from checkerboards. There are also five squares in each block; we'll make them from strips, too.

On page 35 I showed you how to make a single block by cutting sets of triangles like this from a checkerboard. Those ready-made sets of triangles were a big time-saver. You could make four blocks by repeating those steps four times, and I guess you could make a full size quilt by repeating the steps 24 times. But there's a better way as you saw on the diagram on page 47. Sew the triangles and squares together before you cut them out. Then cut out whole sections of the block already made. There are no little pieces to handle, and four blocks can be made with 30 seams instead of 80.

Size of strips and finished blocks

Double-length Alpha strips work nicely in this chapter, so I'll have you start with strips eight times as long as they are wide, plus an inch.

Alpha Strips (Double Length)	Straight Strips	Size of Block
3" x 25"	About 3-1/2" x 14"	About 9"
3-1/2" x 29"	About 4-1/4" x 17"	About 11"
4" x 33"	About 5" x 20"	About 13"

How to make four Ohio Star pillows

Fabric needed:

Light fabric: 1 yd.

Dark (incl.backing): 1-1/2 yds.

Optional:

Scraps of third fabric for centers

2 yds. of fabric for ruffles

2 yds. border fabric with 4 repeats (reduce light fabric to 1/2 yd.)

1. Remove 5" strips from yardage to use later. Lay out the light and dark pieces with right sides together. Fold over, selvages together. Trim off one edge, then

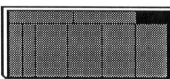

Dark fabric (fabric shown folded)

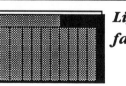

Light fabric

cut, through all four layers, 5" parallel to the selvage. That gives two long strips of each color. Set these aside and continue cutting.

2. Cut Alpha strips. You'll need two light and two dark, 4" x 33". Sew them together.

3. Cut 4" cross sections and **make two 4 x 4 checkerboards.**

4. Turn checkerboards on the bias. The secret of making this block is to turn one checkerboard on the bias by cutting through the **light** squares first. Turn the other one on the bias by cutting through the **dark** squares first. (Remember, the first cut determines which color will be along the edge.)

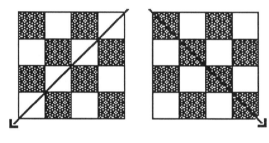

5. Cut two strips of triangles like this from the panel with light along the edge. Measure them.

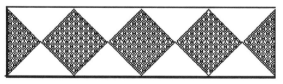

6. Using **long strips** removed in Step 1, cut four strips of dark fabric to match the strips of triangles (about 5" x 20"). Mark as shown on page 50.

7. Sew a dark strip to each side of the patchwork strips. Follow pointers on page 50. (Points match marks, clip off the masses of fabric at points, keep points exactly the same width, etc.)

8. Cut eight cross sections exactly through the points, using your ruler to check seam alignment for accuracy.

9. Choose your center color. Although this is called a "two-color star," you can use a new (third) color for the **centers**. The best way to decide which fabric to use is to arrange four of these strips with different fabric scraps to see which looks prettiest.

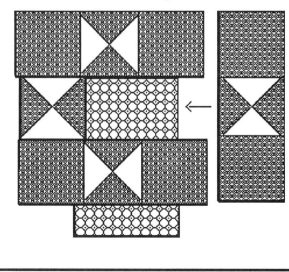

Cut one strip of whichever fabric you choose, the same size as before (about 5" x 20") and mark it in fourths too.

10. Cut two strips of triangles with dark along the edges from the other panel.

11. Sew the center strip between the patchwork strips. Be sure the triangles along one side are aligned with those on the other side. Make one panel.

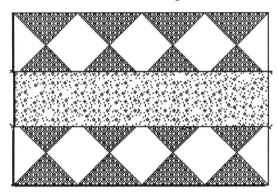

12. Cut cross sections.

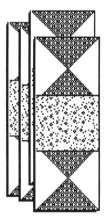

13. Assemble your blocks. Remember the tip on page 35 for keeping points accurate.

14. Cut borders. Press and measure the blocks. (They'll be about 14" square.) Cut remaining light fabric into 3" strips and trim to fit the four blocks.

If you want to add ruffles, fold the extra 2 yards of dark fabric into four layers and cut it all into 5" strips. Make ruffles with usual sewing techniques.

15. Finish pillows. Make backing from remaining dark fabric. Assemble as shown on page 16.

Some other ways to do this project:

- **If you got mixed up** at any point, go back to the directions on page 35. Piece together your blocks from individual triangle sets and squares.

- **Use these blocks for a wall hanging** like the one on page 55; increase the sizes of borders, etc., since these blocks are large and those are small.

- **After making a set of stars with dark backgrounds, try dark stars on light backgrounds.** Just switch lights and darks in the instructions. See the charts on page 62.

- **Use these four blocks for part of a larger project.** For example, make four more blocks and seven plain squares the same size. Join them and add borders to make a **twin bed throw** (about 50" x 72"), similar to the one shown on page 82.

Color Plate 7 illustrates some of these changes. You can see part of a four-block wall hanging with large blocks, dark stars on a light background and a new color in the centers. It is 31" square.

Ohio Star wall hanging

These are smaller blocks, about 9". The finished project is about 27" square. See Color Plate 15.

Small blocks require more accurate sewing, so stick with large blocks if you're not too confident.

Fabric needed:

Light fabric: 1/2 yd.

Dark fabric: 1-1/3 yds.

Batting: 28" sq.

Binding: 4 yds. wide bias tape or 1/4 yd. fabric

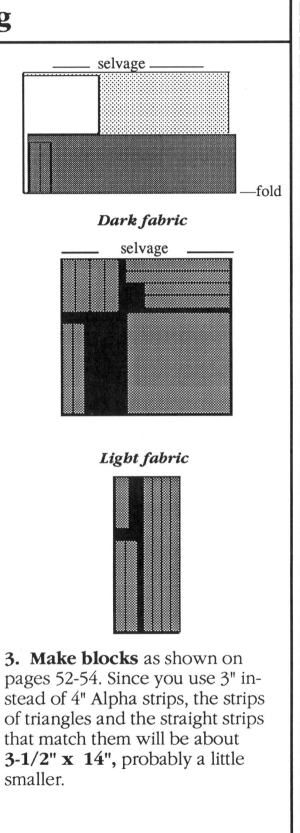

Dark fabric

Light fabric

1. Lay out light and dark fabric, right sides together, with three edges even. Fold over 13", as shown.

2. Cut Alpha strips, 3"x 12-1/2" on fold (3" x 25" when spread out).

3. Make blocks as shown on pages 52-54. Since you use 3" instead of 4" Alpha strips, the strips of triangles and the straight strips that match them will be about **3-1/2" x 14",** probably a little smaller.

4. Add sashing and first borders. Cut four strips 2-1/4" x 44" from the light fabric. Trim to length needed for:

(a) **Sashing between blocks** (two pieces about 9-1/2" long).

(b) **Long sashing** and **top and bottom borders** (three pieces about 19" long).

(c) **Side borders** (two pieces about 22" long).

Use those strips to join blocks into pairs, then into a four-block set. Be careful to keep the seams in one block lined up accurately with those in the block next to it.

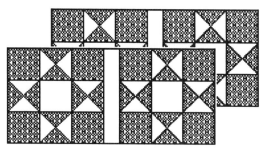

5. Add outer borders. Cut four 4" strips of dark fabric, two about 22" long for the top and bottom borders and two about 28" long for the sides. Plan ahead so you'll have a 28" square of dark fabric for the backing. Sew borders on.

6. Finish project. Cut backing to fit from dark fabric. Add batting and baste layers together. Suggestions: Hand-quilt 1/4" inside seams on each light shape. Quilt hearts in light colored squares if you wish. Bind with wide purchased bias tape or make your own narrow binding.

Another variation

This has dark stars on a light background, a new color for centers and sashing, and one wide border—all are easy changes to make.

Fabric for this variation:

Dark fabric: 1/4 yd.

Light fabric: 3/4 yd.

Backing: 3/4 yd.

The variation shown in Color Plate 7 is described on page 54 since it uses large blocks. You can copy the colors but get a more delicate effect with small blocks.

How to make sets of eight Ohio Star blocks

As I mentioned earlier, you can make almost any project just with 4 x 4 checkerboards, if you make enough of them. But 4 x 8 checkerboards are handier for large projects. Turn them on the bias like this (shown in more detail on page 38).

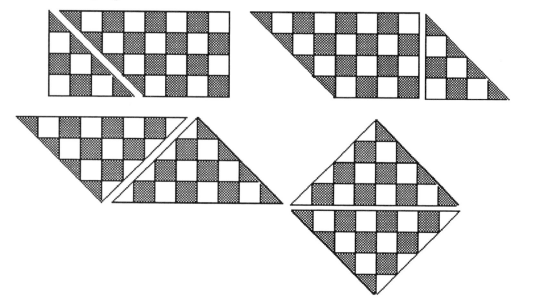

It doesn't matter which direction you cut through **first** when you turn large checkerboards on the bias. When you turned 4 x 4 checkerboards, the panel you made was large enough to cut triangle strips only one direction. But 4 x 8 checkerboards turn to **square** bias panels, and strips can be cut either direction.

Half of the bias panels you make will be cut apart in one direction, half in the other direction.

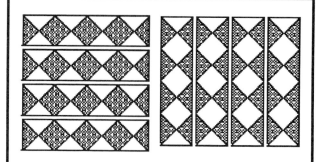

Tip: *Study these strips. All Ohio Star projects use an equal number of each type. These two 4 x 8 panels make all the triangles you need for eight stars.*

Ohio Star baby quilt

This project uses eight small blocks set alternately with seven plain blocks. Finished size is about 37" x 55".

Fabric needed:

Light fabric: 1-2/3 yds.

Dark fabric: 3/4 yd.(can use this for centers too, or use 1/8 yd. of another dark)

Backing: 1-2/3 yds. (enough to bind edges too)

Batting: about 40" x 58"

1. Remove a 13" strip from the light fabric, parallel to the selvage, to use for borders later.

2. Cut Alpha strips: Lay out light and dark fabrics with right sides together. Fold over and cut through four layers. Cut **four strips of light and four of dark, 3" x 25".**

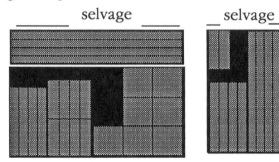

Light fabric   *Dark fabric*

3. Make two 4 x 8 checker-boards.

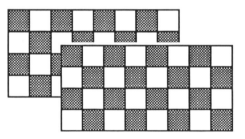

4. Turn checkerboards on the bias. This time it doesn't matter which direction you cut through first.

(overleaf) Hovering Hawks and Split Nine-Patch wall hangings by Christine Kamon of West Chester, PA.

(right) Ohio Star twin throw (page 82) by Estelle Brown of Pasadena, MD, with a special border made of smaller blocks.

(below) Pillows with a Southwest look: Apache block, Indian Plume with a double sawtooth (both page 94), and Five-Patch Pine Tree (page 97).

(left) Six tiny Shoofly blocks (chart on page 110) on Ghee's handbag pattern 851, by Donna McConnell of Searcy, AR. Turtle pincushion by Hmong Craftswomen.

(below) 91″ square Ohio Star project by Sheila Drain of Milton, MA, using 16 blocks, each with its own border. Blue wall hanging (variation of Hovering Hawks on page 131) by Marge Brand of Klamath Falls, OR.

(right) Medallion quilt on wall (page 122) by Sheree McKee of Drayton Plains, MI, is quilted with a commercial quilting machine. On the bed is a not-yet-quilted Ohio Star made by Nathalie Kelly of Fallston, MD, who teaches for Marilyn Isennock.

(below) Modified sampler of Five-Patch blocks by Sandy Even of Leaburg, OR. Wall hanging of four Memory Wreath blocks and sawtooth border (page 154 and Chapter 6) by Margie Bergan of Klamath Falls, OR.

5. Cut one bias panel into four strips, cutting through the **dark** fabric.

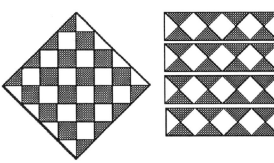

6. Measure those strips. (They'll be about 3-1/2" x 14".) **Cut eight strips of light fabric** to match. Mark them off in fourths (page 50).

Tip: *Review the rules on page 50 before making design panels.*

7. Make four design panels. Sew the strips of triangles to the straight strips like this, matching points to the marks.

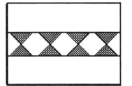

8. Decide which fabric to use for centers. Cut cross sections of the design panel and try different dark fabrics as shown on page 53.

Cut **two strips** of whatever fabric you select (same size as in Step 6). Mark them in fourths too.

9. Cut the other bias panel apart, through light squares.

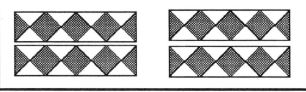

10. Sew strips to the two center strips, like this. Make two of these panels.

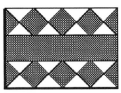

11. Cut cross sections.

12. Assemble eight blocks. Keep points accurate as shown on page 35.

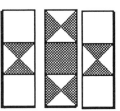

13. Cut seven plain blocks to match patchwork blocks (about 9-1/2"). Assemble all blocks to make quilt top.

14. Add borders. Cut 3" strips from the 13" piece removed in Step 1. Sew in place. Cut cross-grain strips from dark, also 3" wide, for outer border.

15. Finish quilt. See pages 13, 14, and 16, and the suggestions on page 64. Or use your own favorite methods of quilting and binding.

Tip: *To turn the quilt top on the bias as discussed on pages 42-43:*

Make one more star (follow pages 34-35 with 3" x 13" strips) and two plain squares. Make six rows of three blocks each. When turned, the project should be about 50" square. Page 83 will give you an idea of the effect.

Ohio Star queen quilt

This quilt uses 24 large blocks alternating with 25 plain blocks. Size is about 106" square before quilting, considerably smaller after quilting.

Fabric needed:

Light: 7-1/2 yds.   Backing: 9 yds.

Dark: 3 yds.   Batting: 108" sq.

Make a smaller Two-Color Ohio Star project so you know the basic steps before trying this large quilt.

1. Remove a 17" strip from dark fabric and a piece that same size (about 17" x 108") from the light fabric. Set these aside for borders.

2. Cut Alpha strips. For easier handling, remove 66"-67" sections of each fabric to be used now and set the rest aside for later. Spread out the two fabrics, right sides together, and fold over. Cut 12 light and 12 dark strips 4" x 33".

Note: *For Steps 3-8, you may prefer to make one set of eight blocks, then start over for the next set. Directions are for working on all 24 blocks at once.*

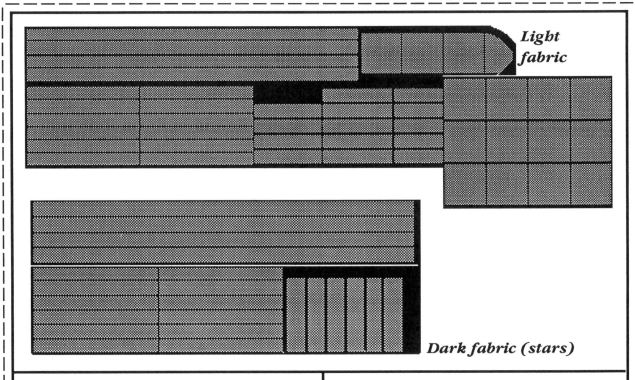

Light fabric

Dark fabric (stars)

3. Make six checkerboards, 4 x 8 size. Turn them on the bias.

4. Cut three panels apart through **dark** squares. Measure strips.

5. Cut 24 strips that size (about 5"x 20") from light fabric. Mark in fourths (see page 50). Make **12 design panels** like this: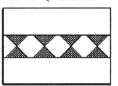

6. Choose fabric for centers as shown on page 53. Cut **six strips** of that fabric and mark them in fourths.

7. Cut remaining bias panels apart through the **light** squares. Assemble with the six center squares into **six design panels:**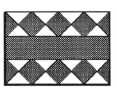

8. Cut cross sections and assemble blocks.

9. Measure finished blocks and cut **25 plain blocks** that size (about 14"). Assemble patchwork blocks and plain blocks into seven rows of seven blocks each (three of one type, four of the other).

10. Add 4" borders from strips removed in Step 1.

11. Make backing (Number 7 on page 15). **Quilt and bind** as you like.

Note: *There are three ways to turn this quilt top on the bias* (see page 42-43 and page 95):

1. Make eight rows of six blocks. The quilt will be long when finished, about 85" x 120".

2. Make eight rows of five blocks. It will be about 85" x 102".

3. Make ten rows of five blocks (make one more star, page 35). It will be about 100" square.

Charts for designing Ohio Star projects

Dark star on light background

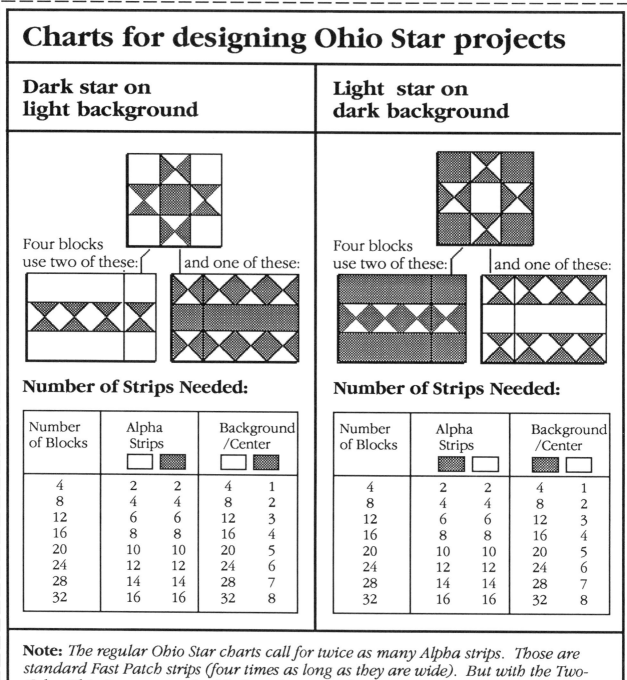

Four blocks use two of these: and one of these:

Number of Strips Needed:

Number of Blocks	Alpha Strips		Background /Center	
4	2	2	4	1
8	4	4	8	2
12	6	6	12	3
16	8	8	16	4
20	10	10	20	5
24	12	12	24	6
28	14	14	28	7
32	16	16	32	8

Light star on dark background

Four blocks use two of these: and one of these:

Number of Strips Needed:

Number of Blocks	Alpha Strips		Background /Center	
4	2	2	4	1
8	4	4	8	2
12	6	6	12	3
16	8	8	16	4
20	10	10	20	5
24	12	12	24	6
28	14	14	28	7
32	16	16	32	8

Note: *The regular Ohio Star charts call for twice as many Alpha strips. Those are standard Fast Patch strips (four times as long as they are wide). But with the Two-Color Ohio Star, we use **double-length strips** (eight times as long as wide).*

Designing your own Two-Color Ohio Star

Use the regular Ohio Star planning and coloring sheet on page 90 to help plan your project.

- **Size of strips:**
Small blocks (8-1/2" to 9"):
Use 3" x 25".
Medium blocks (11"):
Use 3-1/2" x 29".
Large blocks (12-1/2" to 13"):
Use 4" x 33".

Note: *For miniature quilts, use 2" x 17" strips. Make more strips and panels than needed and discard less accurate sections. See Color Plates 15 and 17.*

- **Number of strips to use:** See charts on the page 62.

- **Type of checkerboards to make:**
For **multiples of eight blocks** (8, 16, 24, 32, etc.) make all strips into **4 x 8** checkerboards.
For numbers which are **multiples of 4 but not 8** (4, 12, 20, 28, etc.) make **two 4 x 4** checkerboards, then make all other strips into **4 x 8** checkerboards.

Estimating yardage for large blocks (13")

- **For background color** (triangles and corner squares):

4 blocks	5/8 yd.	16 blocks	2-1/8 yds.	28 blocks	3-5/8 yds.
8 blocks	1-1/8 yds.	20 blocks	2-2/3 yds.	32 blocks	4-1/4 yds.
12 blocks	1-5/8 yds.	24 blocks	3-1/4 yds.		

Calculations are for strips to be cut cross-grain. (You can remove a 3" or 4" strip for borders first.) You can save yardage in big projects by cutting with grain or by using selvage-to-selvage Alpha strips and using leftovers.

- **For star color** (triangles and centers)

4 blocks	1/2 yd.	16 blocks	1-1/4 yds.	28 blocks	2-1/4 yds.
8 blocks	2/3 yd.	20 blocks	1-2/3 yds.	32 blocks	2-1/2 yds.
12 blocks	1 yd.	24 blocks	1-7/8 yds.		

These are also cut cross-grain.

- **For center squares, if you use a third fabric:**

4-8 blocks	1/4 yd.	20-24 blocks	1/2 yd.
12-16 blocks	1/3 yd.	28-32 blocks	2/3 yd.

These are also cut cross-grain.

- **Use charts on page 15 and page 175 to estimate other yardage needed.**

Ideas for Quilting Ohio Star Projects

Ideas on these two pages apply to both Chapter 4 and Chapter 5, so we'll put them between the chapters.

Ideally, you'll chose your quilting method before designing your project. If you'll hand-quilt it, you might choose Variation D or F since they have light backgrounds to show off the quilting. Dark background are better for tying or machine quilting.

If you're tying the quilt, you might make knots at these points. For examples of Ohio Star tied with yarn, see Color Plates 6, 12, and 18.

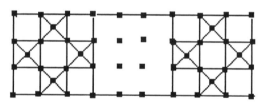

When lap quilting (or machine quilting a small project which can be turned easily), you'll find something interesting about this block. You can start at any point, quilt along all the triangles in the star in one continuous line and end right back where you started.

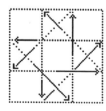

The machine-quilting technique Barbara Johannah describes in her book ***Continuous Curve Quilting*** is quick because you don't have to keep your stitching "in the ditch" (or exactly 1/4" from the ditch). Instead you make gentle curves around the line. Color Plate 9 is an example of this type of quilting with Ohio Star. (This was a fairly small quilt, so it could be turned easily enough to quilt the circles in the plain square.)

If you're machine quilting a large project, try to avoid changes of direction. Here's an easy straight-line quilting plan for a quilt with small blocks alternating with plain blocks:

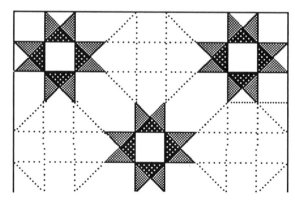

On page 65 is another way to machine quilt a big quilt without much turning.

Machine quilting the Ohio Star with gentle curves

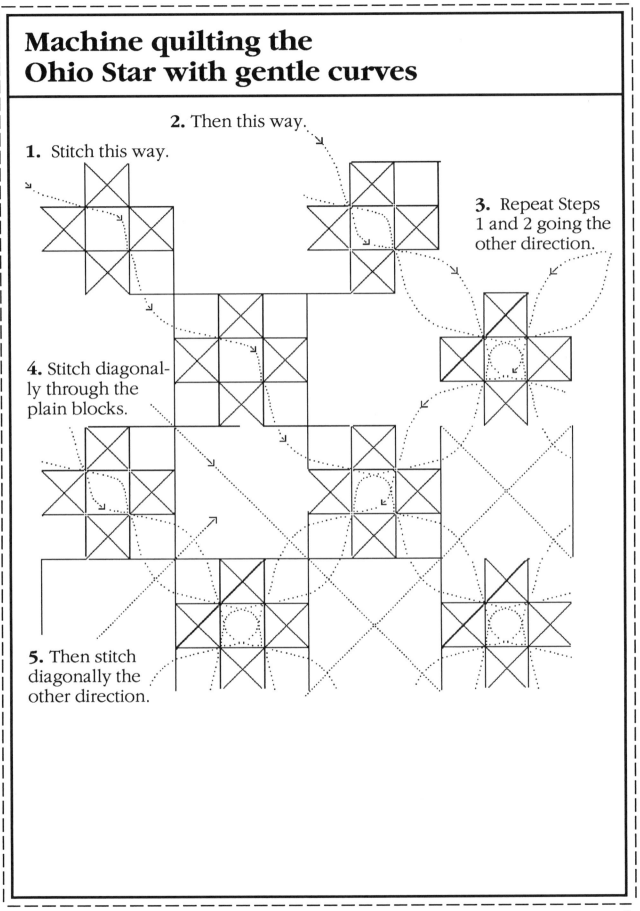

1. Stitch this way.

2. Then this way.

3. Repeat Steps 1 and 2 going the other direction.

4. Stitch diagonally through the plain blocks.

5. Then stitch diagonally the other direction.

5. *The Classic Ohio Star*

A new type of checkerboard

You did Ohio Stars in the last chapter, but we have a big difference now. The inner triangles in these stars are a new color. That extra color is worked into the checkerboard right from the start.

See the sets of triangles hiding in a three-color checkerboard?

The colors in Ohio Star

Here are the terms I will use to designate the colors. Look closely at the star as I describe them, so they'll be clear to you:

Background: The outer **triangles** plus **corners**.
Stars: The triangles that make the **star points**
Accent: The fabric for the **inner triangles**
Center: The checkerboard makes only triangles, so the center color isn't in the checkerboard; it's added later. It can be a new color or repeat one already used.

Although the background color dominates the final block, the star color dominates the checkerboard. There are eight triangles of that color in each block and only four of each of the other two, so you'll

use twice as many strips of the star fabric.

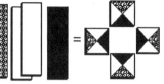

Two sets of strips like these make the triangles for four stars.

The six variations

There are six variations of Ohio Star, shown in pairs:

Variations A and B have **light star points,** and both start with the same type of checkerboard. The **background** in A is the **accent color** in B, and vice versa.

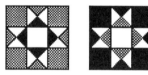

Variations C and D have **medium star points** and start out the same.

Variations E and F have **dark star points** and start out the same.

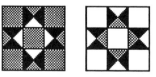

A nifty way to choose fabrics for Ohio Star

You usually make blocks in sets of four or eight. When one block is done, they're all almost finished and it's too late to change your mind about colors. Here's an easy way to visualize your blocks ahead of time.

1. Lay out fabric in this order; **background** fabric on bottom, then **star** fabric, then **accent** fabric, then **center** fabric on top.

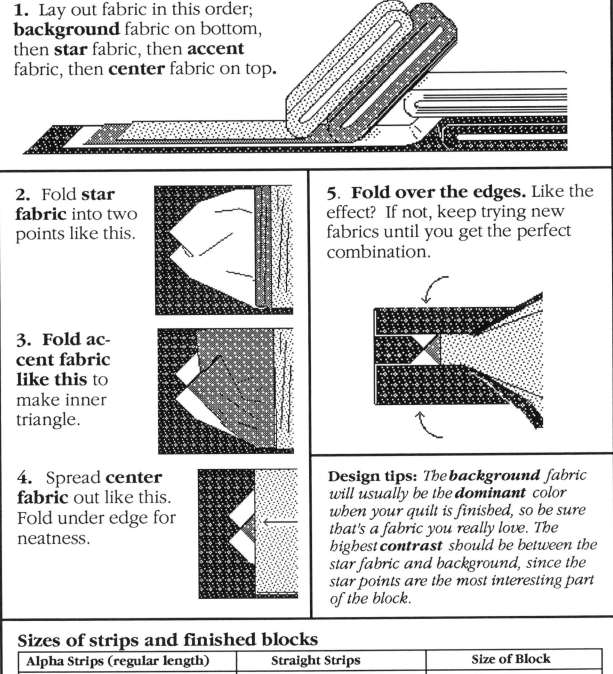

2. Fold **star fabric** into two points like this.

3. Fold accent fabric like this to make inner triangle.

4. Spread **center fabric** out like this. Fold under edge for neatness.

5. Fold over the edges. Like the effect? If not, keep trying new fabrics until you get the perfect combination.

Design tips: *The **background** fabric will usually be the **dominant** color when your quilt is finished, so be sure that's a fabric you really love. The highest **contrast** should be between the star fabric and background, since the star points are the most interesting part of the block.*

Sizes of strips and finished blocks

Alpha Strips (regular length)	Straight Strips	Size of Block
3" x 13"	About 3-1/2" x 14"	About 9"
3-1/2" x 15"	About 4-1/4" x 17"	About 11"
4" x 17"	About 5" x 20"	About 13"

How to get the colors right where you need them

1. Have strips of background and **accent** fabrics alternate with the **star** fabric.

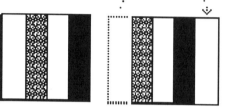

2. Make two types of panels with strips in a slightly different order. Make the first panel, then move the **star** fabric to the other end in the second panel. The background color is on the end of one panel and the accent color is on the end of the other panel.

3. Cut cross sections of the two panels and sew them together to make checkerboards. **Colors go in a stepping up pattern, like this:**

It's the same pattern you find in "Trip Around the World"

It's easy to make that pattern by **mixing up** strips from the two panels, **reversing** some of them as needed. Study this diagram.

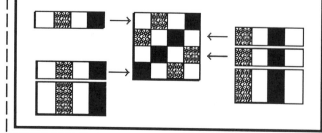

4. "Keep the stars off the steps." Before sewing the last strip on each checkerboard, look at the squares that form the **"steps"** up the **center.** Don't have the **star** fabric (the one with twice as many squares) in this position. You might work with different sizes of checkerboards, but the idea is always the same: Keep the stars off the center steps.

Practice checkerboards

Cut eight strips 4" x 44", two for backgrounds, four for stars, and two for accents. Sew them into two long panels and cut cross sections. Make them into four checkerboards, following the pattern above. (Save the leftovers.)

Be very accurate where all three colors meet. If you have to fudge, do it where only two colors meet.

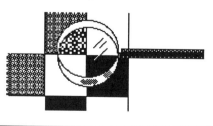

Projects using your practice checkerboards

When you get your practice checkerboards done, decide what to do with them. You can make them into stars for the project on page 82 if you wish.

Or you can leave them in the checkerboard stage and make them into a pretty wall hanging, about 44" square. You can also make more checkerboards and make a large quilt similar to that on page 20. Solid color fabrics in Amish colors or South-west jewel tones would be pretty. Diagonal quilting will complement the designs.

The following two versions have four checkerboards joined by sashing strips.

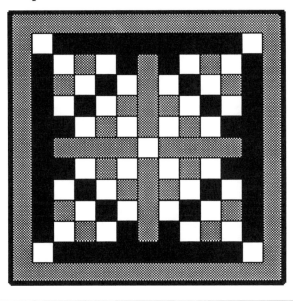

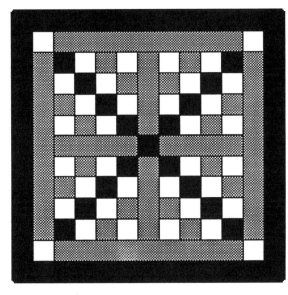

A Trip-Around-the-World effect is achieved in the design at the right. Just use your extra cross sections as the sashing! (You'll need to add a couple of squares, and maybe pick out one or two seams and rearrange squares slightly, to get the colors where you need them.)

Add more borders if you wish.

How to make two blocks

Although we usually work in sets of four or eight blocks, I'm going to show you two blocks first. If you did the practice on page 68, use one of those checkerboards. In fact, you can use your leftover strips if you've already used the four checkerboards. Or use scraps of three fabrics (less than 1/4 yd. of each) and make a 4 x 4 checkerboard now.

For small projects, make your checkerboards from regular Alpha strips (**four times as long as they are wide**, plus an inch). Most projects in this chapter use 13" blocks, which start with 4" x 17" Alpha strips.

1. Cut four 4" x 17" strips (one stack, as shown on page 71).

2. Sew strips to each other. Remember how I said you needed two slightly different panels? That's if you're going to make sets of four or eight blocks, but we're going to make only two blocks, so we'll take a shortcut.

Instead of making two panels, by "moving the star fabric to the other end" on the second one, we're going to move **half** the star fabric to the other end on just **one** panel. So cut one strip into two 8-1/2" pieces first and sew them like this:

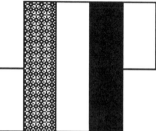

3. Cut cross sections. Make a 4 x 4 checkerboard. Remember, "Keep the stars off the steps." Pick out the last seam if you forgot.

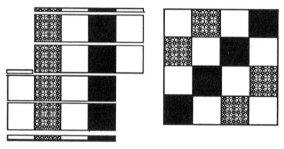

4. Turn the checkerboard on the bias.

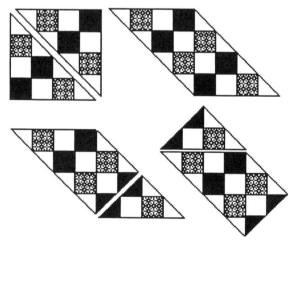

5. Cut the bias panel apart into sets of triangles as shown below.

Measure the triangle sets (about 5"). Cut **squares** to match, eight of the background fabric and two of the star fabric (or a new fabric) for the centers.

Tip: *See page 35 for tips on lining up the points accurately.*

Piece together two blocks.

A good cutting method for small Ohio Star projects:

1. Spread out **background** fabric, **right side up.**

Spread **star** fabric over it with two edges even, **right side down.** Then fold the star fabric up over itself to make two layers (right side is now **up** on top layer).

2. Spread **accent** fabric on top, **right side down,** again lining up edges evenly.

3. Now you have two layers of star fabric, one layer of background and one layer of accent. You can cut stacks of strips with right sides together in pairs, ready to sew without adjusting.

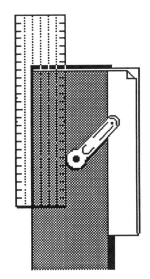

How to make a set of four blocks

1. Cut Alpha strips. Lay out fabric as shown on page 71. Cut two stacks, making **two** strips of background and accent fabric, **four** of star fabric.

2. Sew strips together in the special pattern. Cut cross sections and make two checkerboards. Remember not to use the star fabric for the center squares.

3. Turn only one checkerboard on the bias. Cut through **the star fabric** first because that's the fabric you need on the **long** edges of the first panel.

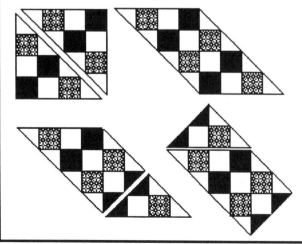

If you accidentally cut the wrong direction, set it aside for Step 9. Cut the the reserved checkerboard the correct way and you're back on track.

4. Cut the bias panel into two strips. Measure them. (They'll be about 5" x 20", maybe a little less.)

5. Cut four strips that size from the background fabric. Mark each of them in fourths by folding and cutting notches.

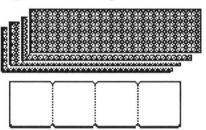

6. Make two panels like this, by sewing background strips to patchwork strips. Match points to the notches.

Remember to keep blunt points equally blunt (about 5/8").

7. Cut the panels into eight cross sections.

Cuts should go exactly through the **centers** of the blunt points. And the **seams should line up** with the lines on the ruler, including the **45° angle** marks. Can't line things up? Pick out a few inches of seam, ease a point over a bit, and resew.

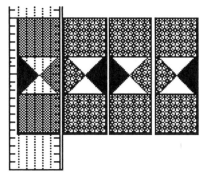

8. Choose the fabric for the center squares. Even if you already bought fabric, feel free to change your mind. You need only a little fabric, so use the prettiest one you can find. Lay four of these strips over one fabric, the other four over another fabric. Keep trying new fabrics until you find the absolutely perfect one.

In Step 11 you'll cut a strip of this fabric for the centers. You might change your mind again before then. That's okay.

9. Turn the other checker-board on the bias. This time cut first through the **background** fabric or **accent** fabric (whichever is in the corner squares).

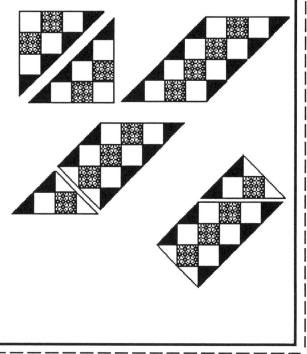

It doesn't matter whether the background color or accent color is along the edge of the panel.

10. Cut that panel into two strips now. Study the patchwork strips as you clip the points. They have the **star** fabric in the center, the **background** fabric along one edge, the **accent** fabric along the other.

11. Cut one strip of center fabric to match (use the same measurement used in Step 5). Mark it off in fourths as before. Pin the **center** strip between the patchwork strips, making sure the **accent** color is the one touching the center strip. (Place a cross section from Step 7 along the end to double-check.) Sew strips together, following the craftsmanship guidelines given on page 50, especially the one about lining up triangles on one side of the panel with triangles on the other side.

12. Cut cross sections.

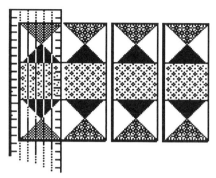

13. Assemble your blocks.

Don't fret: Do you feel there are too many new ideas? Did you goof when turning the second checkerboard on the bias? Steps 10 to 12 are optional. They are most useful when making dozens of blocks for a large quilt. You may choose to just cut sets of triangles and piece them together with individual squares as before to assemble your block.

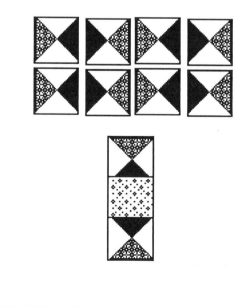

Four-block Ohio Star wall hanging

This is Variation B, made with 9" blocks. Size will be about 30"-36" square, depending on the borders used.

Fabric needed:

Background: 1/3 yd.

Star points, sashing, first borders: 1/2 yd.

Accent triangles: 1/8 yd.

Centers: 1/8 yd.

Borders: 1 yd. of border print with four repeats of **two** nice borders

No cutting diagrams are given. Cut all strips across grain, except the borders.

1. Cut Alpha strips, **3" x 13"**, from fabric folded as shown on page 71. Total strips needed: two for background, four for stars, and two for accent triangles.

2. Follow basic steps on pages 72-74, using 3" cross sections to make checkerboards.

3. Cut four background strips, about 3-1/2" x 14". They'll be **dark** instead of medium. **Center strip** will be light. Panels will look like this:

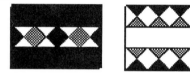

4. Assemble the blocks.

5. Add sashing and first borders. Cut remaining **star color** into three strips 1-1/2" wide. Divide into shorter strips as needed:

• Two strips the size of blocks (about 9-1/2") to join blocks in pairs.

• Three strips (about 19") for sashing and top and bottom borders.

• Two strips (about 21"-22") for side borders.

6. Add more borders, using desired border prints and mitering corners.

7. Cut backing to fit and **quilt and bind** with your favorite methods.

You can use this as the center in a larger quilt as shown in Color Plate 22. See Chapter 6 for ideas on doing the sawtooth borders.

How to make a set of eight blocks

You could just make lots of 4 x 4 checkerboards and make projects four blocks at a time, but I think it's easier to work with larger panels and make eight blocks at a time. Here's how to do it with **regular length Alpha strips** (four times as long as they are wide, plus an inch):

1. Cut Apha strips: four of **background** fabric, eight of **star** fabric, and four of **accent** fabric.

2. Sew them together into two panels, alternating the star fabric with the other two and making the two panels slightly different, as before.

3. Cut cross sections and combine into one **8 x 8 checkerboard** with colors arranged as in the small checkerboard. (Watch the star color.)

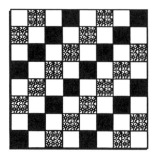

4. Turn checkerboard on the bias as shown on page 77.

5. Cut the bias panel in half. Use the two parts like this:

Make four of these panels:

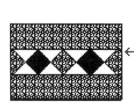

Make two of these panels:

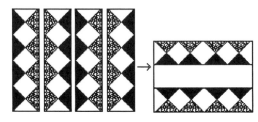

6. Cut cross sections and make blocks as usual.

It may have occurred to you that you could use **4 x 8 checkerboards** for this block. Of course you can. You'll get a square bias panel which you'll cut apart as above. You can also make panels from **double-length Alpha strips.** I'll show you some advantages to that on page 81.

As you can see, there are several ways to achieve the same results. Study the whole system and decide on your favorite ways. Often you may think you've made a mistake but then find you haven't, as you'll see on page 78. And if you do make a mistake, there's usually a way out, as you'll see on pages 79 and 80.

How to turn an 8 x 8 checkerboard

The 8 x 8 checkerboard is turned on the bias in exactly the same way as the 4 x 4 size. This time, it doesn't matter which way you cut first.

1. Cut diagonally from any corner.

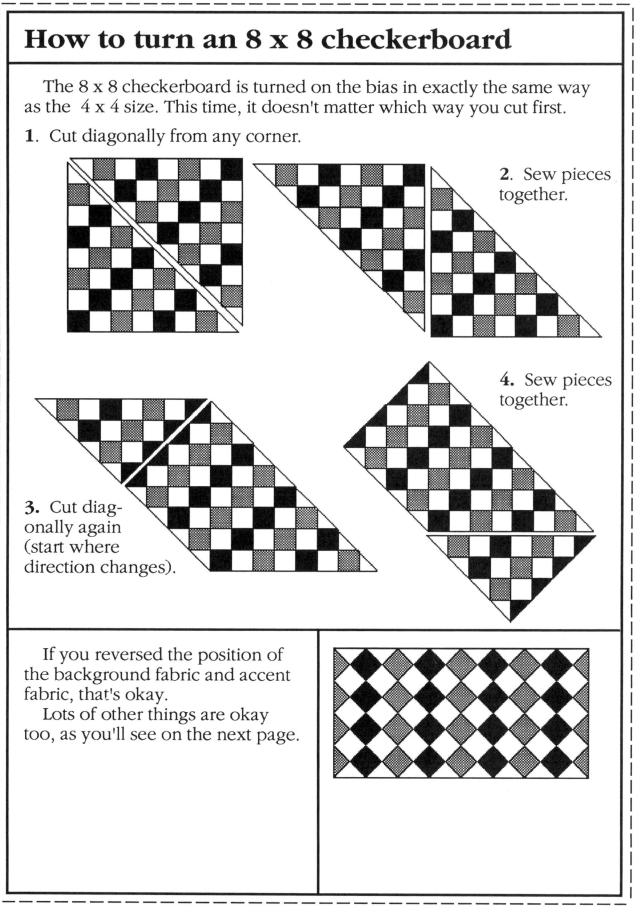

2. Sew pieces together.

4. Sew pieces together.

3. Cut diagonally again (start where direction changes).

If you reversed the position of the background fabric and accent fabric, that's okay.

Lots of other things are okay too, as you'll see on the next page.

Did you goof? (Probably not)

If your work doesn't look quite like the drawings on page 77, it's probably still okay. Your colors slant the other direction? That's okay.

1. You cut the other way because you're left-handed? That's okay.

2. You put the two halves together in a slightly different arrangement? That's okay, as long as the colors are still orderly.

3. You cut off this end instead of the other? That's okay.

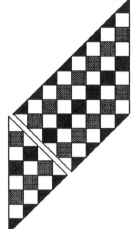

(It's even okay if you cut off **both** ends. As you saw on page 76, you'll cut the bias panel in two later anyway. Just sew the two **triangle** pieces to each other so they match the other piece.)

4. Finish the bias panel like this. Colors progress the opposite direction from the panels on page 77. If background and accent colors are reversed (lower drawing), that's okay too.

If you did goof

Not **everything** is legal. Look at this checkerboard. The **star** color goes up the center steps! (You can tell it's the star color, because there are twice as many of those squares.)

That definitely is **not** okay. Pick out a seam and sew the last strip to the other end, **or** use this trick:

1. Don't start your diagonal cut from the **corner**; cut through the square next to it (the one which **should** have been in the corner).

2. Sew the pieces together. It looks strange with that square where there should be a triangle.

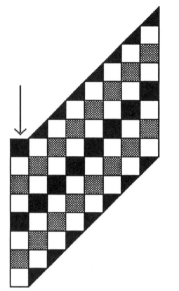

So cut off a triangle and sew it where it belongs. Then go on to Steps 3 and 4 on page 77.

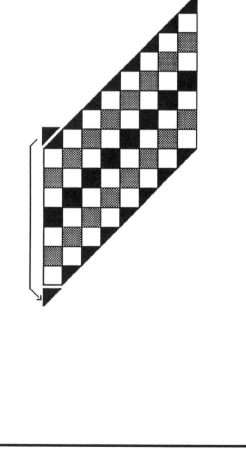

What to do if the star fabric is in the wrong position

In spite of all my warnings, do you have the star color going down the center of your checkerboard? I've done that myself and know how much trouble it causes. The colors just aren't in the right position.

If the star fabric is in the wrong position, When you cut triangle strips, they look like this:

And sets of triangles you cut look like this (16 of each):

Well, when life deals you lemons, make lemonade:

1. Make Two-Color Ohio Stars.

You'll make at least two types of stars and you can make a big assortment of them if you start getting creative with the centers. Just cut out 32 sets of triangles and 40 squares (32 for back

grounds and eight for centers). Piece blocks together individually. See Chapter 4 and pages 35 and 37.

2. Make five regular stars. If

you catch your mistake before cutting strips of triangles, cut off the outside rows, all around the panel. Discard these (or use them for Fast Patch projects from Chapter 7). Cut the remaining panel into three-color sets of triangles. You can make 21 sets but need only 20. Cut **25 squares** that same size (20 for background squares, five for centers). Piece together individually.

3. Pretend you were never intending to make Ohio Stars.

Sew three-color sets of triangles together like this:

Add big background triangles of your original background color. Eureka! Pinwheels! (Eat your hearts out, all you people who didn't read this paragraph because you never make mistakes.)

Working with extra-long strips

Extra-long (44") strips are quick to make. Leftover cross sections can be made into checkerboards for extra blocks if you wish.

One way: Cut eight full-length strips. Sew four strips into one panel and cut off two sections of normal strip length (17" for large blocks, 13" for small blocks). Sew them together to make one panel and proceed as usual.

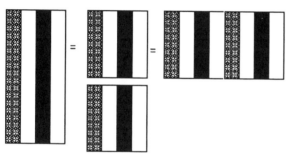

Repeat with the other four strips (sewn in slightly different order as usual.)

Make **extra blocks** from the leftover ends. One cross section from each panel makes a 2 x 4 checkerboard which makes one block:

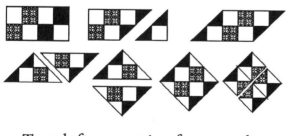

Two leftover strips from each panel make two blocks. See page 71. Four leftovers from each panel make four blocks.

Another way: For 16 blocks, you can sew full length strips into two giant panels like this. Use the cross sections to make two big checkerboards.

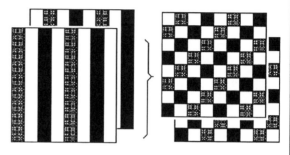

Again, use the leftovers. With large blocks, pick out a couple of seams and put together two 4 x 4 checkerboards. With small blocks, you'll have enough leftovers to make a third 8 x 8 checkerboard!

Ohio Star twin-bed throw

This throw is made of eight large blocks, Variation B, set with seven plain blocks, about 50" x 72". For examples of this project see Color Plates 4 and 9.

Fabric needed:

Dark (Background, plain blocks, outer border): 2-1/2 yds.

Light (Stars and centers): 2/3 yd.

Medium (Inner triangles, first border): 3/4 yd.

Backing: 3 yd.

Batting: 54" x 76"

1. **Cut Alpha strips,** 4" x 17", four of dark and medium fabric, eight of light fabric. (Leave them full length if you wish.)

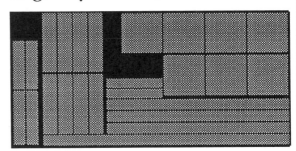

Dark fabric (background)

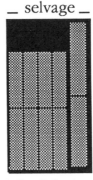

Light fabric
(stars)

Medium fabric
(accent)

2. **Make an 8 x 8 checkerboard** and turn it on the bias. Cut it in two. (Or make two 4 x 8 checkerboards, or four 4 x 4 checkerboards.)

3. **Cut strips of triangles with light along the edges.** Measure and cut **eight dark strips** to match. (Try to leave a 4"-5" strip along the selvage for borders to avoid some piecing.) Make four panels like this:

4. **Choose fabric for centers.** Cut two strips.

5. Cut strips of triangles the other direction (with background fabric along one edge and accent fabric along the other edge). Sew them to the center strips, making two panels like this:

6. Cut cross sections and assemble eight blocks.

7. Cut seven squares of dark fabric to match blocks. (They'll be about 13-1/2".) Assemble blocks and plain squares like this:

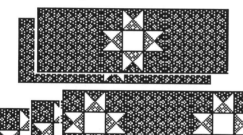

8. Make inner borders. Cut six strips 3" wide from **medium** fabric. Piece strips as needed and sew in place.

9. Make outer borders. Cut remaining **dark fabric** into 4" strips lengthwise. Piece to fit quilt and sew in place.

10. Make backing. Use Number 1 on page 15. **Quilt and bind** with your favorite technique.

Ohio Star double-bed quilt

To more than double the size of the quilt, make 17 stars and 18 plain blocks. Arrange in seven rows of five blocks each. Will be about 82" x 108". See Color Plate 13.

Fabric needed:

Background, plain blocks, borders: 4-2/3 yds.

Stars, border: 1-7/8 yds.

Accent triangles, border: 1-1/2 yds.

Centers: 1/3 yd.

Backing: 6 yds. (see No. 5 on p. 15)

Batting: 90" x 108"

Tip: *To turn the whole quilt top on the bias (page 42):*

Smaller quilt: Make one more star and two more plain squares. Make six rows of three blocks. When turned, quilt will be about 65" square.

Larger quilt: Only 16 stars needed. Make eight rows of four blocks each. When turned, quilt will be about 86" square.

Here's what Ohio Star looks like set diagonally.

Ohio Star queen coverlet or double spread

Here's a popular size of quilt, 30 large blocks set with sashing the same color as the accent triangles. Finished size is about 97" x 108" before quilting. Variation A is shown, but you can substitute other variations. Look at the Color Plates for ideas, choose fabrics as shown on page 67, and then find the chart which matches your darks and lights. Be familiar with the basic Ohio Star steps before starting this project.

Fabric needed:

Backgrounds, border (medium in the art work): 4-1/4 yds.

Star, border (light in the art work): 2-1/2 yds.

Accent, sashing, border (dark here): 4 yds.

Centers: 2/3 yd.

Batting: 98" x 110"

Backing: 8-1/3 yds. (See Number 6 on page 15.)

Directions for 30 blocks: I'll have you use double-long strips and use the leftover cross sections to make more blocks; you'll save fabric that way. (If you prefer to go by the charts on page 86, making 32 blocks instead of 30, get an extra half-yard of the first three fabrics.)

1. **Cut Alpha strips,** 4" x 44": six of **background** and **accent fabric,** 12 of **star fabric.** (Or use regular length strips, the number given on the charts.)

2. **Make checkerboards:**

(a) Make two 8 x 8 checkerboards, as shown on the right side of page 81. Make two 4 x 4 checkerboards from the leftovers.

(b) Make one 8 x 8 checkerboard, as shown on the left side of page 81. Make a 4 x 4 checkerboard from the leftovers.

(If cutting strips as shown on charts, make four 8 x 8 checkerboards.)

3. **Make blocks as usual.** Use 30 (or 32) strips for backgrounds and eight for centers. Follow the cutting layouts so you leave long sections for making borders. Some strips may be cut into individual squares to piece last few blocks.

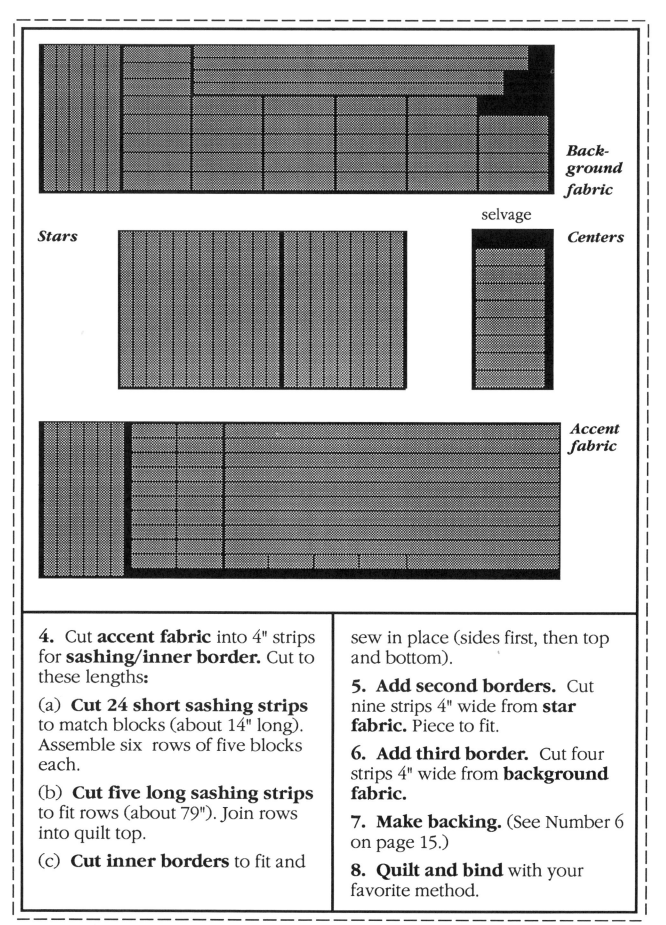

Background fabric

Stars

selvage

Centers

Accent fabric

4. Cut **accent fabric** into 4" strips for **sashing/inner border.** Cut to these lengths:

(a) **Cut 24 short sashing strips** to match blocks (about 14" long). Assemble six rows of five blocks each.

(b) **Cut five long sashing strips** to fit rows (about 79"). Join rows into quilt top.

(c) **Cut inner borders** to fit and sew in place (sides first, then top and bottom).

5. Add second borders. Cut nine strips 4" wide from **star fabric.** Piece to fit.

6. Add third border. Cut four strips 4" wide from **background fabric.**

7. Make backing. (See Number 6 on page 15.)

8. Quilt and bind with your favorite method.

Charts for designing Ohio Star projects

Variation A

Four blocks use two of these: and one of these:

	Number of Strips Needed				
No. of Blocks	Alpha Strips*			Background/ Centers	
4	2	4	2	4	1
8	4	8	4	8	2
12	6	12	6	12	3
16	8	16	8	16	4
20	10	20	10	20	5
24	12	24	12	24	6
28	14	28	14	28	7
32	16	32	16	32	8

*(Use half as many if double-length strips.)

Variation B

Four blocks use two of these: and one of these:

	Number of Strips Needed				
No. of Blocks	Alpha Strips*			Background/ Centers	
4	2	4	2	4	1
8	4	8	4	8	2
12	6	12	6	12	3
16	8	16	8	16	4
20	10	20	10	20	5
24	12	24	12	24	6
28	14	28	14	28	7
32	16	32	16	32	8

*(Use half as many if double-length strips.)

Both **A** and **B** use this unit, so they start the same.

Sew strips together in this order.

This must be dark or medium fabric, not light!

Variation C

Four blocks use two of these:

and one of these:

No. of Blocks	Number of Strips Needed				
	Alpha Strips*			Background/ Centers	
	■	▨	□	■	▨
4	2	4	2	4	1
8	4	8	4	8	2
12	6	12	6	12	3
16	8	16	8	16	4
20	10	20	10	20	5
24	12	24	12	24	6
28	14	28	14	28	7
32	16	32	16	32	8

*(Use half as many if double-length strips.)

Variation D

Four blocks use two of these:

and one of these:

No. of Blocks	Number of Strips Needed				
	Alpha Strips*			Background/ Centers	
	□	▨	■	□	⬚
4	2	4	2	4	1
8	4	8	4	8	2
12	6	12	6	12	3
16	8	16	8	16	4
20	10	20	10	20	5
24	12	24	12	24	6
28	14	28	14	28	7
32	16	32	16	32	8

*(Use half as many if double-length strips.)

Both **C** and **D** use this unit, so they start the same.

Sew strips together in this order.

This must be dark or light fabric, not medium!

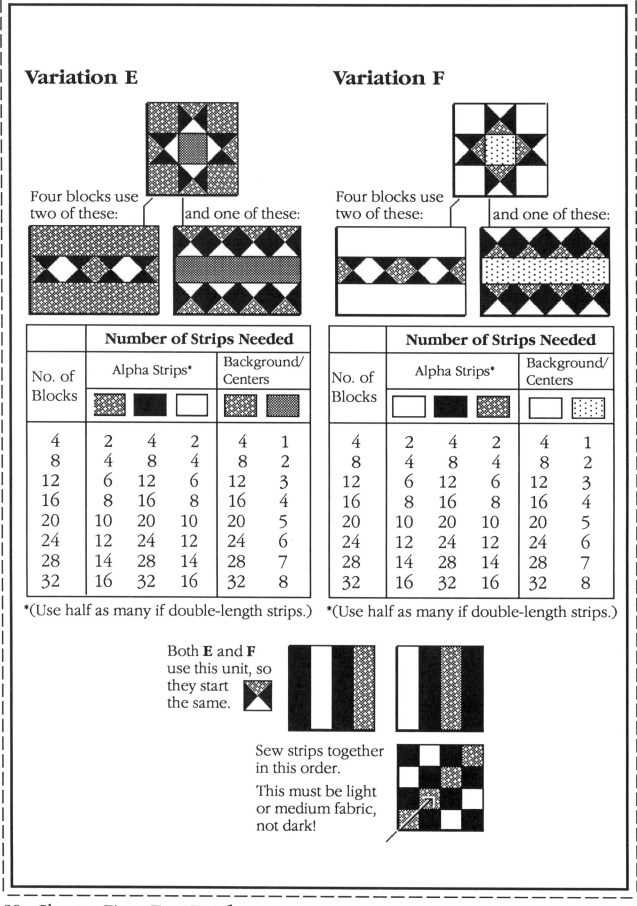

Variation E

Four blocks use two of these: and one of these:

Number of Strips Needed

No. of Blocks	Alpha Strips*			Background/ Centers	
4	2	4	2	4	1
8	4	8	4	8	2
12	6	12	6	12	3
16	8	16	8	16	4
20	10	20	10	20	5
24	12	24	12	24	6
28	14	28	14	28	7
32	16	32	16	32	8

*(Use half as many if double-length strips.)

Variation F

Four blocks use two of these: and one of these:

Number of Strips Needed

No. of Blocks	Alpha Strips*			Background/ Centers	
4	2	4	2	4	1
8	4	8	4	8	2
12	6	12	6	12	3
16	8	16	8	16	4
20	10	20	10	20	5
24	12	24	12	24	6
28	14	28	14	28	7
32	16	32	16	32	8

*(Use half as many if double-length strips.)

Both **E** and **F** use this unit, so they start the same.

Sew strips together in this order.

This must be light or medium fabric, not dark!

Designing classic Ohio Star projects

Size of strips:
Normal length: Use 3" x 13" strips for small blocks (9").
Use 3-1/2" x 15" strips for medium blocks (11").
Use 4" x 17" for for large blocks (13").
Double-length: Use 3" x 25" strips for small blocks (8-1/2" to 9").
Use 3-1/2" x 29" strips for medium blocks (11").
Use 4" x 33" for for large blocks (13").
Number of strips: See the charts on pages 86-88.
Colors to use : See page 67 for a way to visualize your block and choose fabric. Then find the variation that matches your dark/light pattern on charts.

Estimating yardage for large blocks

1. Yardage for background triangles and corner squares, for 13" blocks only:

4 blocks	1/2 yd.	16 blocks	1-2/3 yds.	28 blocks	2-3/4 yds.
8 blocks	7/8 yd.	20 blocks	2 yds.	32 blocks	3-1/4 yds.
12 blocks	1-1/4 yds.	24 blocks	2-1/2 yds.		

Strips are cut cross-grain. You can remove a 3" or 4" strip for borders first. Save yardage in big projects by cutting selvage-to-selvage Alpha strips and using leftovers (page 81).

2. Yardage for star points, large blocks:

4 blocks	1/3 yd.	16 blocks	1 yd.	28 blocks	1-3/4 yds.
8 blocks	1/2 yd.	20 blocks	1-1/4 yds.	32 blocks	2 yds.
12 blocks	3/4 yd.	24 blocks	1-1/2 yds.		

3. Yardage for accent triangles, large blocks:

4 blocks	1/4 yd.	16 blocks	1/2 yd.	28 blocks	1 yd.
8 blocks	1/4 yd.	20 blocks	2/3 yds.	32 blocks	1 yd.
12 blocks	1/2 yd.	24 blocks	3/4 yds.		

4. Yardage for centers, large blocks:

4-8 blocks	1/4 yd.	20-24 blocks	1/2 yd.
12-16 blocks	1/3 yd.	28-32 blocks	2/3 yd.

See charts on page 15 to estimate backing fabric and page 175 to estimate sashing, plain blocks, and borders.

Planning sheet for Ohio Star

Use this sheet to design your quilt, to calculate yardage, and to keep your fabrics in the right place in the panels.

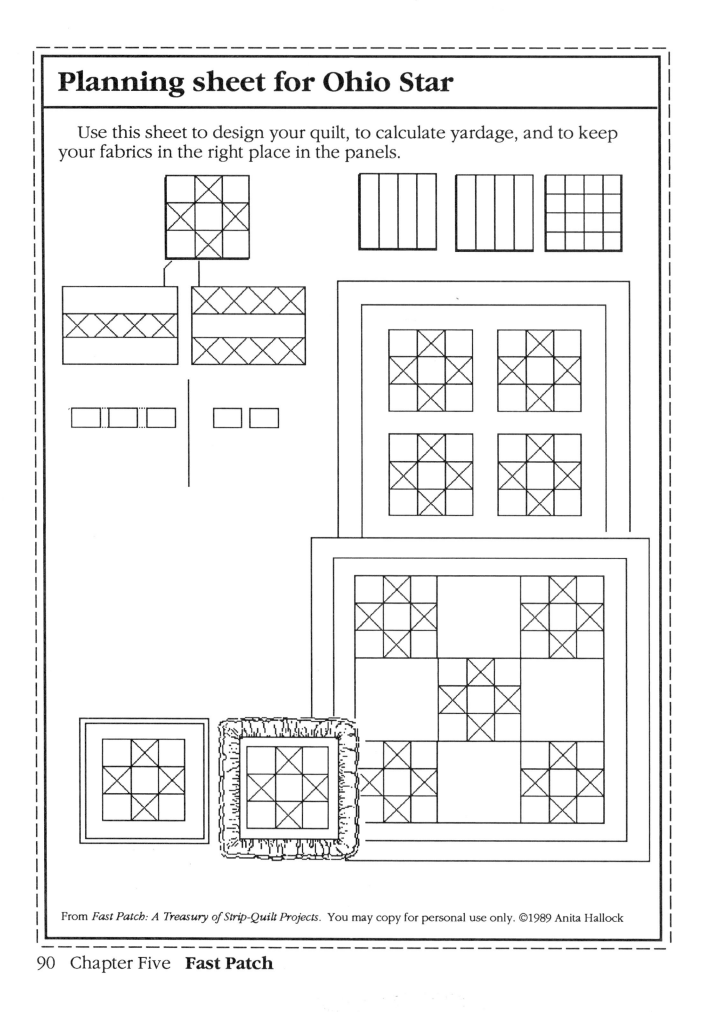

(overleaf) On the wall, experimental Five-Patch sampler made by Christine Kamon of West Chester, PA, for her daughter. On the chair, two variations of Two-Color Ohio Star. Miniature blocks by Judy Siccama of the Tail End Workshop in East Haven, CT. Blue project by Anita Hallock. Stove and rocker owned by Ben and Alice Bloomer.

(above) "Windy Days" by Ida Copeland of Ann Arbor, MI—large Shoofly blocks with surprises in the alternate blocks. Hand-quilted by Lizzie Schmucker.

(left) Miniature Two-Color Ohio Star by Christine Kamon, who teaches at Grandmother's Patches in Uwchland, PA. This unusual arrangement has eight blocks with a light background and a center block with a dark background.

(below) Blue-and-white Ohio Star by Peggy Brintle of Mt. Airy, NC, for her grandson. Since the sashing is the same color as the background in the blocks, the contrasting squares are very important.

(right) The Five-Patch sampler was made and machine-quilted by Cherie Teuscher of Fall Creek, OR. The 36″ Crown of Thorns wall hanging was made and hand-quilted by Geb Jones of Klamath Falls, OR. See page 162 for Crown of Thorns B chart; see Chapter 6 and page 154 for sawtooth borders. Both projects were made from 4″ Alpha strips.

(below) Machine-quilting on this Sister's Choice C block shrunk Anita Hallock's queen-size quilt from 95″ × 105″ to 84″ × 96″. Directions on page 142.

6. *Sawtooth Chains*

You know now how to make checkerboards and turn them on the bias so you can cut strips of triangles. The rest of the book will deal with strips like this:

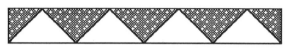

They have **four large triangles** of one fabric and **three large and two small** triangles of another fabric.

One common way these strips are arranged is lined up with the triangles facing each other. Then you can cut off ready-made **sawtooth chains**. You can make sawtooth chains by the yard to embellish complete quilts, make blocks featuring sawtooth chains, or just make some pillow tops with sawtooth borders.

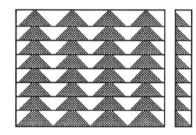

Marking the centers

The first thing you need is a way of marking the triangles so the **point** of one triangle is sewn exactly to the **center** of the triangle in the next tier. The key is to mark the centers of all triangles

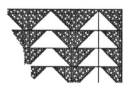

ahead of time by drawing lines through the bias panel. (Don't worry about using disappearing ink or anything. You'll cut through those places later.)

You could mark the centers with **cuts**, if you prefer. They show up on both light and dark fabric, both right and wrong sides of the fabric.

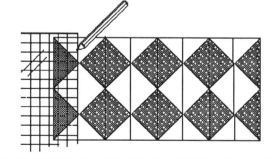

Important: *Mark in one direction and make your next cut in the **other** direction.*

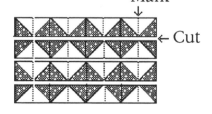

The slant of the triangles

When in a chain, triangles slant **up** or they slant **down.** You can't change the slant by turning the chain upside down; you just change the side the dark triangles are on. You **can** change the slant by turning the chain on its side, and that's useful sometimes.

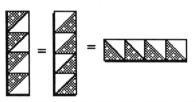

You automatically have an **equal number** of **uphill** and **downhill** slants, whether you want them or not. If there is a definite direction to the triangles, you make two different blocks.

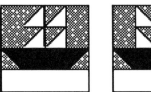

How to make attractive corners

Sawtooth chains make great borders. But the **corners** of borders might not turn out pretty if you don't plan ahead. Here are three ways to make nice corners:

Make a pair of "revolving" borders:

One 4 x 8 checkerboard makes enough for two good-sized pillows.

1. Measure the sides of the project, including **one corner,** but not both.

2. Sew enough rows of strips together to equal that measurement. In this case, all eight rows are used. Remember to match the points of one row to the marks made in the next row. Keep points of the triangles equally blunt.

3. Cut into chains.

4. Make two sets of borders. Use all of the uphill chains in one set and all the downhill chains in the other.

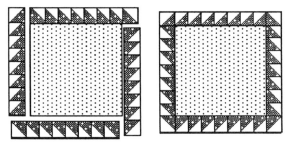

Make switch-in-the-centers borders:

1. Measure project.

2. Sew together enough rows to make up **half** the distance of one side, not counting the corner triangle. Keep points nicely aligned and equally blunt.

3. Sew on half a strip of triangles for the corners. Why **half?** The top and bottom borders don't need corners but side borders do.

Note: *On pages 98-101, you'll see how to put this type of border around quilts of any size.*

4. Cut chains.

5. Piece together as shown.

6. Sew to project. Use shorter chains for top and bottom borders, longer ones for sides.

Add sawtooth borders to a diagonal project:

1. Do Steps 1-3 above.

2. Sew on a plain strip (1" or more wider than the strips of triangles). Sew to end where colors contrast.

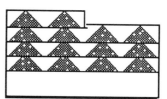

3. Cut chains.

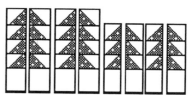

4. Sew chains to large background triangles.

5. Trim ends, making triangles as shown.

6. Sew to project. The extra inch or so in Step 2 often helps fill in the extra space so parts will all fit together.

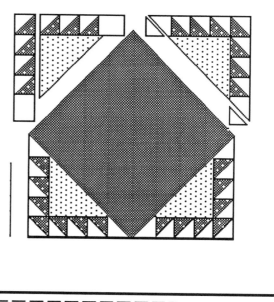

Use squares in the corners

This time we'll put borders around smaller squares to make Navajo quilt blocks like those shown on Color Plate 10.

1. Make a panel like this (use a 4 x 4 checkerboard from 5" Alpha strips).

2. Cut chains.

3. Measure the short chains. Cut two squares from one of your fabrics* to match the **length** (8" to 8-1/2") and four small squares of that same fabric to match the **width** (about 3-1/8").

4. Sew chains and squares in place as shown, first the short ones, then the longer ones. Turn chains upside down or on their sides so all triangles slant the same direction.

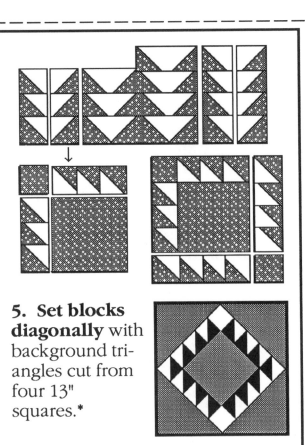

5. Set blocks diagonally with background triangles cut from four 13" squares.*

You can make two different pillows by varying the fabrics used for the squares and background triangles.

Double sawtooth quilt

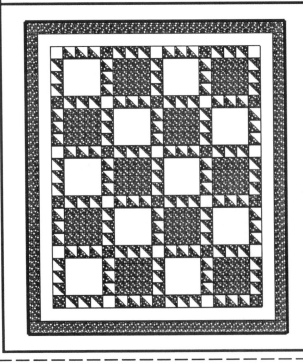

This 56" x 67" quilt has two different blocks, each with sawtooth chains on only two edges. The blocks share their sawtooth edges.

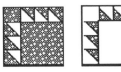

Fabric needed:

Dark: 2-1/8 yds.

Light: 2-1/8 yds.

Backing: 3-1/2 yds.

Batting: 58" x 70"

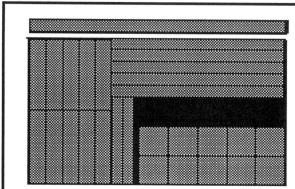

Both fabrics

1. Remove 3" strips from both fabrics to help make borders.

2. Cut Alpha strips, cross-grain, 10 strips of light and 10 of dark, 5" x 20-1/2" (you can leave them double-long).

3. Make checkerboards, two 4 x 8, one 4 x 4.

4. Turn checkerboards on the bias, mark centers, and cut strips of triangles as usual.

5. Cut two light and two dark strips that match the strips of triangles; they'll be about 3-1/8" x 25". Sew straight strips and triangle strips together as shown below, making **two of each panel.** Cut leftover triangle strips in two and make small panel:

6. Cut panels into chains. Measure the shorter chains (triangles only). Cut **20 squares** that length (about 8"), 10 from light and 10 from dark.

7. Piece together 20 blocks. All triangles in this quilt must slant the same direction. You get that effect by turning half the chains on their sides. See box below.

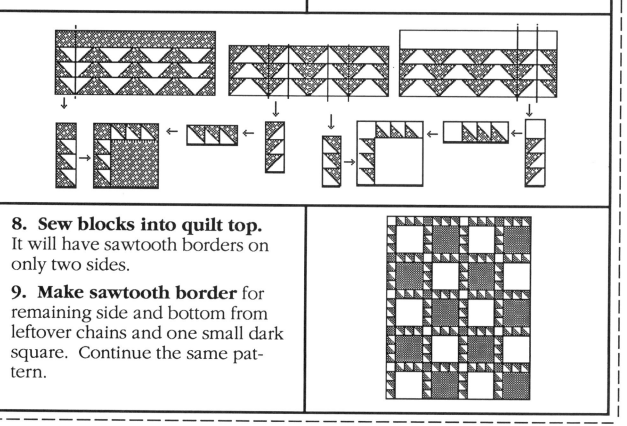

8. Sew blocks into quilt top. It will have sawtooth borders on only two sides.

9. Make sawtooth border for remaining side and bottom from leftover chains and one small dark square. Continue the same pattern.

10. Make borders. Cut remaining fabric into 3" strips lengthwise and piece strips together to make outer borders.

11. Making backing. See Number 1 on page 15. **Quilt and bind** with favorite methods.

Simplified Feathered Star

This oversized Feathered Star block combines a two-color Ohio Star, pages 34 and 35, and four blocks like those in the Double Sawtooth quilt. It will be about 21" square plus borders. Use it as the center of a medallion quilt or as a wall hanging.

1. Make sawtooth blocks first. Use a 4 x 4 checkerboard made with 4" strips. Turn it on the bias, mark centers, and cut strips of triangles as usual.

2. Sew three strips of triangles together. Sew on a half length straight strip (about 2-1/2" x 10").

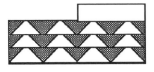

3. Cut chains.

4. Sew chains to four light squares that match the shorter chains (about 6-1/2" square).

5. Make star points (see page 35) from Alpha strips 5-1/2" x 23". Trim triangle sets to your measurement in Step 4 (about 6-1/2" square). Add 2-1/2" background strips that same length of light fabric to the light side of each set.

6. Add a center square. Assemble the star.

More ideas for using sawtooth chains

I don't have room to give directions for these blocks. Do some experimenting with them after you've tried some of the pillows. There are probably hundreds of different blocks that use sawtooth chains.

Try designing your own tree. Draft your own templates for a trunk and base (or adapt patterns you already have; tree templates are quite easy to alter to fit your sawtooth chains). See Color Plates 10 and 26 for conventional trees with Fast Patch sawtooth "branches."

The trees and baskets shown here are compatible with the Five-Patch blocks in Chapter 8, if you like samplers.

Or try a basket block.

My favorite use for sawtooth chains is making borders. In the next few pages I'll give you charts and ways to calculate borders for any size project.

Calculations for sawtooth borders

Determine the size of borders you'll need, then use this chart to get started. All sizes are approximate. Need more triangles? Make another small checkerboard. These sawtooth diagrams are for borders that change directions in the middle; figures under the panels give the number of rows used. Fit borders to your quilt as shown on pages 100-101.

Bold numbers = 5" Alpha strips,
Light numbers = 4" Alpha strips

Total Inches	Checkerboard	Square Borders	Rectangle Borders
Size 1 **86"** (61")	**4 x 4**	**22" square** (15") 3 & 4	**22" x 27"** (15" x 19") 3 & 5
Size 2 **130"** (91")	**4 x 6**	**32" square** (23") 5 & 6	**27" x 38"** (19" x 27") 5 & 7
Size 3 **173"** (122")	**4 x 8**	**43" square** (30") 7 & 8	**38" x 49"** (27" x 34") 6 & 10
Size 4 **216"** (152")	**2 x 4 +** **4 x 8**	**54" square** (38") 9 & 10	**48" x 65"** (34" x 46") 8 & 12
Size 5 **259"** (182")	**4 x 4 +** **4 x 8**	**65" square** (46") 11 & 12	**59" x 76"** (42" x 53") 10 & 14
Size 6 **302"** (213")	**4 x 6 +** **4 x 8**	**76" square** (53") 13 & 14	**70" x 86"** (49" x 61") 12 & 16

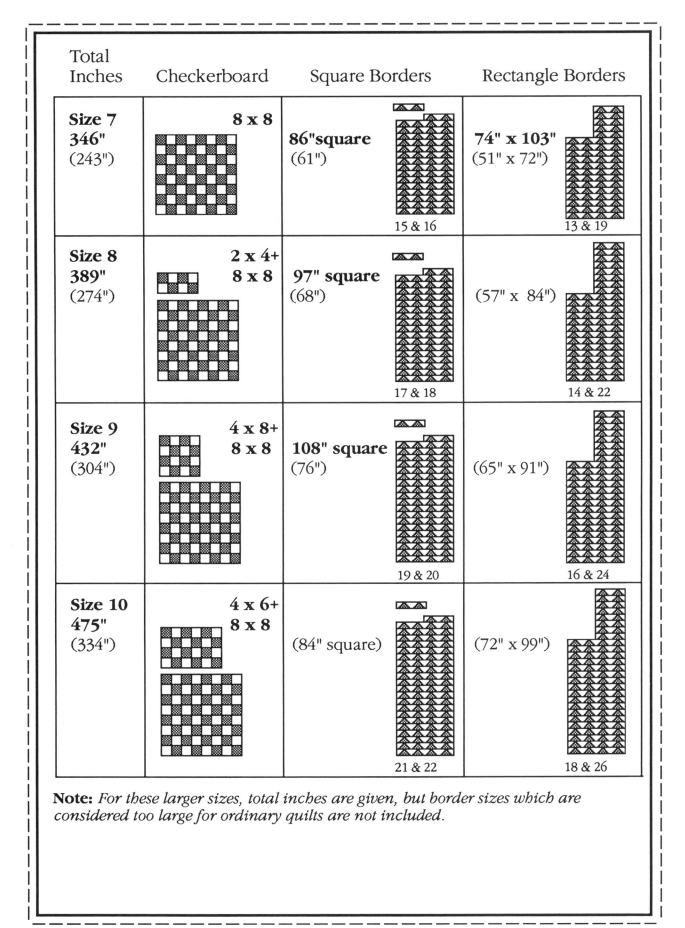

Total Inches	Checkerboard		Square Borders	Rectangle Borders
Size 7 **346"** (243")		**8 x 8**	**86"square** (61") 15 & 16	**74" x 103"** (51" x 72") 13 & 19
Size 8 **389"** (274")		**2 x 4+** **8 x 8**	**97" square** (68") 17 & 18	(57" x 84") 14 & 22
Size 9 **432"** (304")		**4 x 8+** **8 x 8**	**108" square** (76") 19 & 20	(65" x 91") 16 & 24
Size 10 **475"** (334")		**4 x 6+** **8 x 8**	(84" square) 21 & 22	(72" x 99") 18 & 26

Note: *For these larger sizes, total inches are given, but border sizes which are considered too large for ordinary quilts are not included.*

How to make sawtooth borders for your project

1. Decide on the size of triangles for your border. If you made blocks from Chapters 6-8, match the triangles in your blocks. But if you made Ohio Star with 4" strips, use **5" Alpha strips** for the borders.

  If you made Ohio Star with 3" strips, use **4" strips**.

2. Make the **border** just before the sawtooth border **extra wide** if possible (see Step 10).

3. Measure your project. Use the charts on pages 98-99 to find **how many checkerboards** you'll need. Go by the total inches around your project or use "Square" or "Rectangle" border sizes if they match fairly close.

4. Make the checkerboards. Turn them on the bias and mark the centers.

5. Cut strips of triangles and begin sewing them together. Keep adding rows until your panel fits **half the distance** on the short end (seam allowance lines up with the halfway point). **Trim** the border to fit the sawtooth border if needed.

Note: *You'll have to press the panel to get it flat enough to measure against the quilt top, but try not to stretch it out of shape. If possible, press it thoroughly with spray starch, then let it sit overnight to ease back into shape.*

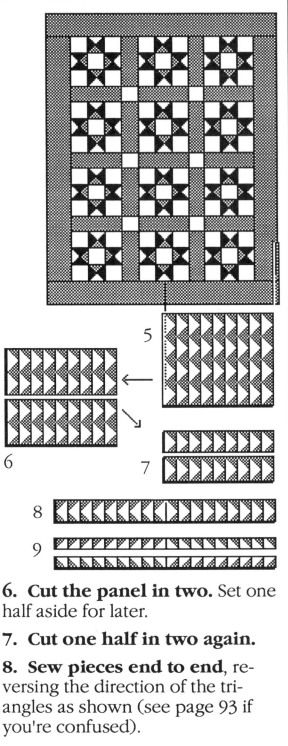

6. Cut the panel in two. Set one half aside for later.

7. Cut one half in two again.

8. Sew pieces end to end, reversing the direction of the triangles as shown (see page 93 if you're confused).

9. Cut the long piece in two again.

Note: *You now have the sawtooth borders for the two **ends** of your quilts. Don't sew them on yet, however! Read Steps 10 and 11 first.*

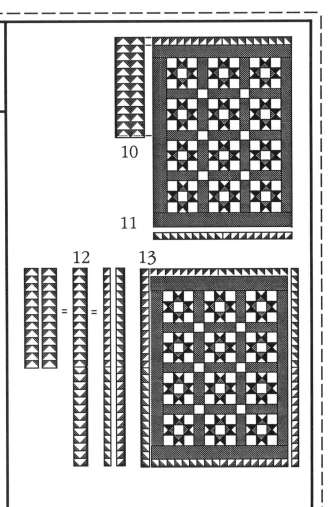

10. Make the side borders.
(You may have to make end borders **narrower** to fit side triangles, so don't sew sawtooth borders on the **end** yet!)

Cut remaining strips of triangles in half and continue lengthening the panel as before until it fits half the distance of the side, including the end sawtooth which you haven't added yet.

11. Trim the end borders, if needed, so triangles come out even. Sew end borders on.

12. Divide panels and resew as you did in Steps 7, 8, and 9.

13. Sew side borders in place.

You can get away with **stretching** a bias sawtooth chain to fit a long edge, but don't **ease** it. The quilt will shrink somewhat in quilting. A border which is stretched a bit might actually be flatter when the quilting is done, while one that is eased may ruffle around the edges.

Design tip: *What should you do if triangles still don't come out even? You may see some old quilts that have parts of the end triangles just whacked off, but you can't get away with that. I prefer putting in another narrow border to enlarge the quilt slightly.*

7. *Magic Little Blocks*

Beta strips

For the double sawtooth blocks in Chapter 6, you cut straight strips and attached them to the strips of triangles so that chains would have **squares** on the end. The blocks in Chapters 7 and 8 have lots of squares mixed up with the triangles, so I'm going to use a new term to describe the strips that make them: **Beta strips**. Beta means "second," and these strips are cut in the second cutting session.

Beta strips are cut exactly the same size as strips of triangles, eight times as long as they are wide. (Do **not** add an inch for good measure as you did for the Alpha strips. These Beta strips are exactly the right size so you can ease the bias strips to fit them and avoid stretching.)

Beta width will often be used for sashing and borders.

The Ohio Star blocks used straight strips to make squares, too, but they weren't called Beta strips because they were extra wide.

Sizes of strips and blocks

Here are common measurements for projects in Chapter 7. Sizes vary because some people's seams are 5/16" or 3/8". **The numbers in bold print are theoretical; the sizes I see most often have an asterisk by them.** The most important numbers are the **Beta sizes.** Once you find yours, you may want to circle them.

Strips which become triangles: **"Alpha Strips"** (4 times as long as wide, plus 1")	Strips which become squares: **"Beta Strips"** (8 times as long, match triangle strips)	**Final Piece** (see p. 173)	Block size	
			Grid of 3: Shoofly Snowball Split 9-Patch	**Grid of 4:** Sailboat Hovering Hawks
4" x 17"	**2-1/2" x 20"** or 2-3/8" x 19"* or 2-1/4" x 18"	**2"** scant or 1-7/8"* or 1-3/4"	**5-3/4"** or 5-5/8"* or 5-1/4"	**7-3/4"** or 7-3/8"* or 7"
5" x 21"	**3-1/4" x 26"** or 3-1/8" x 25"* or 3" x 24"	**2-3/4"** or 2-5/8"* or 2-3/8	**8-1/4"** or 7-3/4"* or 7-1/4"	**11"** or 10-1/2"* or 10"
6" x 25"	**3-7/8" x 31"** or 3-3/4" x 30"* or 3-5/8" x 29"	**3-3/8"** 3-1/8" or 3"	**10"** 9-3/8"* or 9"	**13-3/4"** or 12-1/2"* or 12"

Panels and strips used for Shoofly block

Compare this chart with the one on page 47. The steps look the same until Step 7. Blocks in this chapter use the narrower strips of triangles used for sawtooth chains. And there's a new term for the strips added in Step 8, "Beta strips." (See page 102.) Small blocks are usually made in sets of eight at a time.

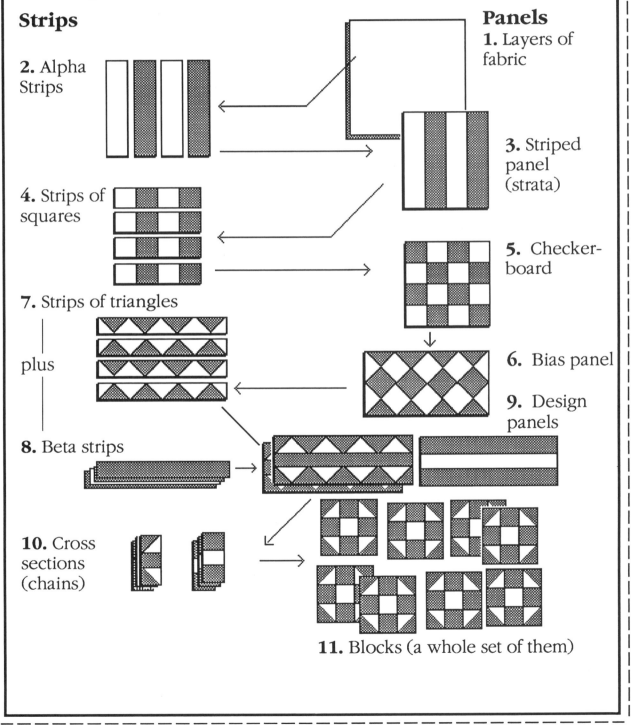

Strips

2. Alpha Strips

4. Strips of squares

7. Strips of triangles

plus

8. Beta strips

10. Cross sections (chains)

Panels

1. Layers of fabric

3. Striped panel (strata)

5. Checker-board

6. Bias panel

9. Design panels

11. Blocks (a whole set of them)

Review these ideas before starting Chapter 7

You may have skipped around a little to get to this chapter. That 's okay, if you'll now review these pages to make sure you haven't skipped any important ideas:

• Chapter 1 for basic quiltmaking, and for charts for sashing and backing.

• Page 17 for tips on making checkerboards.

• Page 33 for why we turn checkerboards on the bias.

• Page 34 for how to turn 2 x 4 checkerboards on the bias.

• Page 36 for how to turn 4 x 4 checkerboards on the bias.

• Page 38 for how to turn 4 x 8 checkerboards on the bias.

• Page 42 for ideas about turning a whole quilt top on the bias.

• Page 48 for an explanation of terms like Alpha strips and design panels.

• Pages 49-50 for special rules for working with bias strips and design panels.

• Page 91 for how to mark centers of triangles for accurate alignment. (You'll need to mark centers for most of the blocks in this chapter.)

These first few pages give important things about blocks in this chapter, so read them thoroughly, too. Here's one more important rule:

Marking Beta Strips

To evenly ease the strips of triangles (which are on the bias) to these straight strips, mark the Beta strips in eight even sections (or at least four). You can fold and notch them if making only a few, or stack and cut slashes along the edges with an X-acto knife. Then match the points of the triangles and center marks (page 91) to these marks.

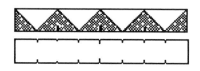

The size of the triangles

When you made Ohio Star, the triangles turned out surprisingly large because the diagonal measurement of a square is longer than the horizontal measurement. You could use fairly small Alpha strips.

When you made sawtooth chains, the triangles turned out surprisingly small because each of those triangles was cut one more time and another set of seams were taken. That's the way it is with blocks from now on.

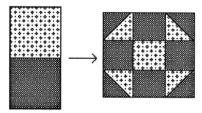

See page 173 to learn more about sizes of final triangles.

The little blocks in Chapter 7

When you mix squares and triangles, you can make hundreds of interesting blocks. The blocks in this chapter are small but fun to work with because you can combine them with each other and with Nine-Patch blocks from Chapter 2 to get some interesting effects.

"Three-Patch" or "Nine-Patch"?

If you made a block with just two strips, it could be called either a "Two-Patch" or a "Four-Patch" (the name used on page 22). I won't give you blocks this small, but I'll use these motifs in larger blocks in Chapter 8.

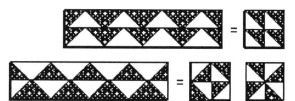

Our next blocks will be made from three strips, so I like the term "Three-Patch." But others call them "Nine-Patch." In fact I'll have to keep the name Nine-Patch and Split Nine-Patch because those are recognized names.

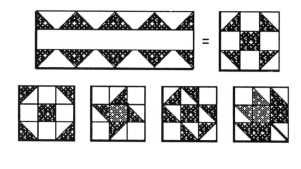

Blocks presented later in this chapter, the Sailboat and the Hovering Hawks, will be "Four-Patch," (or Sixteen-Patch).

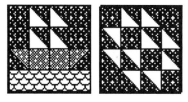

Blocks presented in Chapter 8 will be "Five-Patch" (or "Twenty-Five Patch"—that term tells you why I prefer the smaller numbers; some blocks might be called "144-Patch" if you continue that logic).

Why the disagreement over terms? Because ladies who were making quilts all over the country a hundred years ago didn't get together for conventions to vote on what to call their blocks.

Most of the blocks in this chapter are from my earlier book, *The Magic of Fast Patch,* but you'll find some new things, too.

The Shoofly block

The Shoofly block is one of the oldest blocks, but Grandma never made it like this. Here are the panels you'd use for four blocks. Charts are on pages 110 and 111. See Color Plate 11 for a beautiful bag using six tiny Shoofly blocks. (Projects I'll give you won't use blocks that small, but you can try them on your own later.)

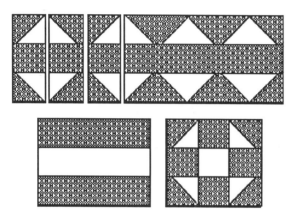

What's okay and what isn't?

Until you have done a lot of Fast Patch, you may not know whether you have something correct or not if your work doesn't quite match the diagrams.

If the diagram looks like this:

Is this okay?

Yes, because the cross sections will look the same.

Is this okay?

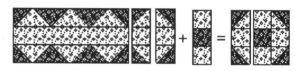

No, because the cross sections don't make a Shoofly block.

They do, however, make a Snowball block, and that's a legitimate block, too. Sometimes new blocks are invented when you goof up but don't want to pick out seams or throw away things. (But do try to follow the diagrams, because you can't always count on creating a pretty block if you goof.)

The Snowball block

Snowball charts are shown with the Shoofly charts because the blocks are so closely related (see pages 110 and 111). The Snowball block alternates well with the Nine-Patch block (see page 108) and is used in the medallion quilt on page 122.

Shoofly wall hanging

This is the green project shown on the front cover. The finished size is 37" square.

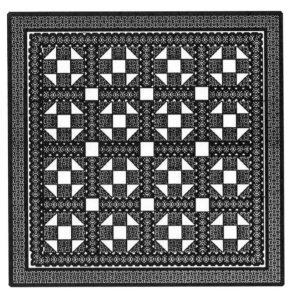

Fabric needed:

Dark: 1 yd.

Light: 1/2 yd.

Border print: 2 yds. with 4 repeats (or 1 yd. if there are 2 suitable borders)

Backing: 1-1/8 yds.

Batting: 38" square

No cutting diagrams are given; just cut all strips cross-grain (except borders).

1. Cut Alpha strips: four light and four dark, 4" x 17".

2. Make a 4 x 8 checkerboard.

3. Turn it on the bias and mark centers (page 91).

4. Cut strips of triangles. Measure them (they'll be about 2-3/8" x 19").

5. Cut Beta strips to match, eight dark and four light. Mark them (page 104).

6. Make design panels as shown on page 111 (Shoofly B). You'll need six panels.

7. Assemble 16 blocks.

8. Make sashing. Choose border print. Cut 24 pieces of sashing as long as the blocks (about 6") and nine light squares the same width as the sashing. Assemble as shown above. Add first border, either of same border print or a closely related one. Miter corners.

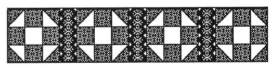

9. Add outer borders. Cut four borders, up to 4" wide, from dark fabric.

10. Layer with backing and batting. Quilt and bind with your favorite method.

Nine-Patch combinations in a crib quilt

Part of the magic of this chapter comes from combining blocks to make new effects. For this crib quilt, choose a combination of Nine-Patch A and Snowball A (back diagram) or Nine-Patch A and Shoofly A (front diagram). Size is about 42" x 57".

I prefer to have a quilt symmetrical from side to side and from top to bottom, but I compromised on this one because the blocks come in sets of eight. Construction was easier for 30 blocks (15 of each).

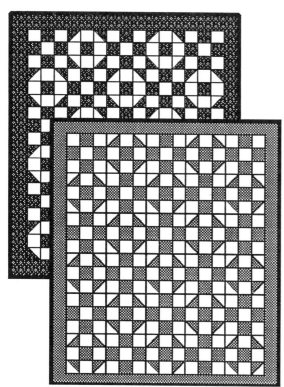

Fabric needed:

Light: 1-1/2 yds.

Dark: 1-1/2 yds.

Backing: 1-2/3 yds.

Batting: 45" x 60"

No cutting layouts are given. Cut all strips lengthwise for this one.

1. Remove a 13" strip parallel to selvage from dark fabric. Set aside for borders.

2. Cut Alpha strips. Spread out light and dark fabric with selvages even. Fold end to end and cut two stacks of strips, 5" x 21" (four of each fabric). Leave fabric undisturbed for next cutting session.

3. Make a 4 x 8 checkerboard.

4. Turn checkerboard on the bias, mark centers (page 91), and cut into strips.

5. Cut Beta strips to match (about 3-1/8" x 25"), 18 light and 10 dark.

6. Make design panels, following diagrams on pages 32 and 110.

7. Make blocks. You'll have 16 of each but will use only 15.

8. Assemble quilt top, making six rows of five blocks each as shown.

9. Add 3" borders cut from dark strip removed in Step 1 (remove selvage first).

10. Layer backing, batting and quilt top, and trim to fit.

11. Quilt and bind as you prefer.

Shoofly/Nine-Patch double-bed quilt

This quilt is sort of a doubled version of the project on page 108, but it's much larger because it uses large-scale blocks made from 6" Alpha strips. There are 32 Shoofly A and 32 Nine-Patch A blocks. (You can use Snowball instead of Shoofly, of course.) The project is about 76" x 95".

Fabric needed:

Dark fabric: 3-2/3 yds.

Light fabric: 5-1/3 yds.

Backing: 5-1/2 yds.

Batting: 80" x 98"

See the cutting layout at the bottom right.

1. Remove 13" strip along selvage of both light and dark fabric for borders.

2. Cut Alpha strips, 6" x 25". You'll need eight light and eight dark.

3. Make two 4 x 8 checkerboards. Turn checkerboards on the bias, mark centers and cut strips as usual.

4. Cut Beta strips (about 3-3/4" x 30"): 20 from dark fabric, 36 from light.

5. Make design panels, following charts on pages 32 and 110. You'll need 24 panels; you may want to complete some sets of blocks before making all the panels.

6. Make blocks. You need 63, so you'll have one extra. **Assemble quilt top,** making nine rows of seven blocks each.

7. Cut borders using strips from Step 1. You can make 3" wide borders in dark, and up to 6" borders in light. You can have either light or dark fabric next to the design.

8. Make backing. See Number 3 on page 15. **Quilt and bind** with your favorite methods.

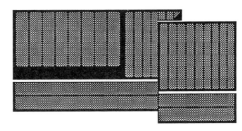

The cutting layout is basically the same for dark and light fabric, but you need more light strips.

Shoofly and Snowball charts

Shoofly A

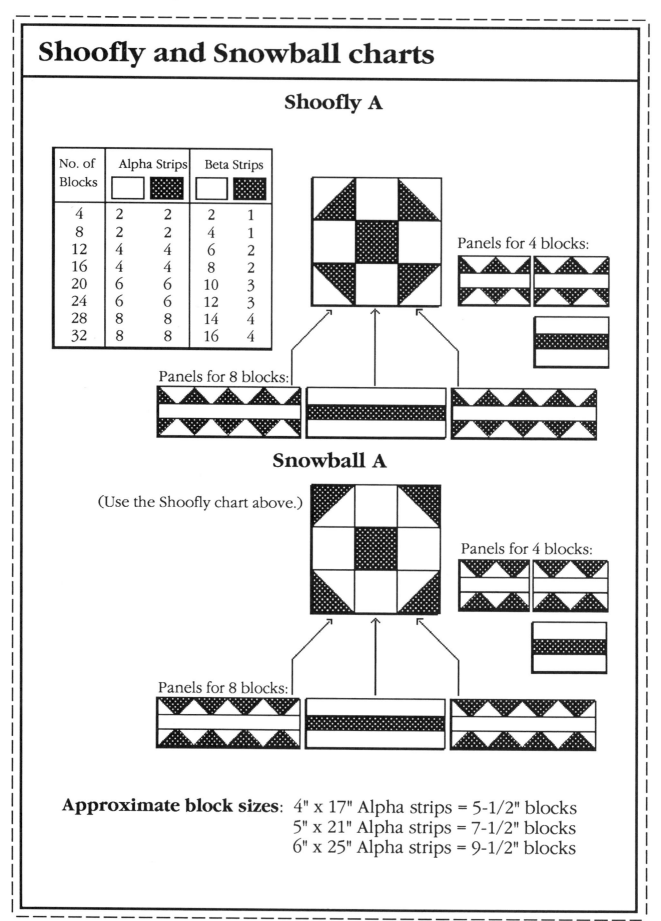

No. of Blocks	Alpha Strips		Beta Strips	
4	2	2	2	1
8	2	2	4	1
12	4	4	6	2
16	4	4	8	2
20	6	6	10	3
24	6	6	12	3
28	8	8	14	4
32	8	8	16	4

Panels for 4 blocks:

Panels for 8 blocks:

Snowball A

(Use the Shoofly chart above.)

Panels for 4 blocks:

Panels for 8 blocks:

Approximate block sizes: 4" x 17" Alpha strips = 5-1/2" blocks
5" x 21" Alpha strips = 7-1/2" blocks
6" x 25" Alpha strips = 9-1/2" blocks

Shoofly B

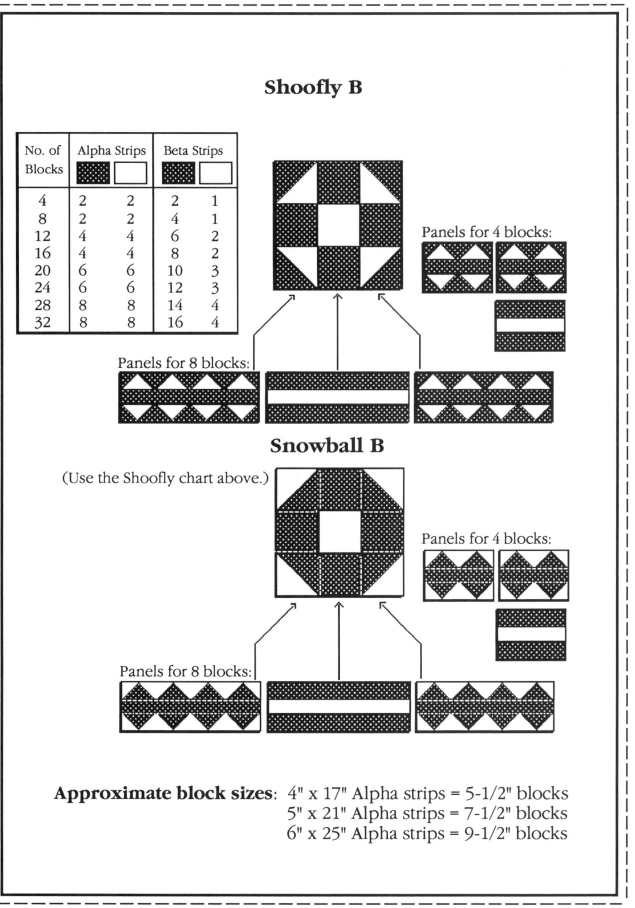

No. of Blocks	Alpha Strips		Beta Strips	
4	2	2	2	1
8	2	2	4	1
12	4	4	6	2
16	4	4	8	2
20	6	6	10	3
24	6	6	12	3
28	8	8	14	4
32	8	8	16	4

Panels for 4 blocks:

Panels for 8 blocks:

Snowball B

(Use the Shoofly chart above.)

Panels for 4 blocks:

Panels for 8 blocks:

Approximate block sizes: 4" x 17" Alpha strips = 5-1/2" blocks
5" x 21" Alpha strips = 7-1/2" blocks
6" x 25" Alpha strips = 9-1/2" blocks

The Split Nine-Patch block

Two types of triangle strips are used for this block, with darks and lights in opposite positions.

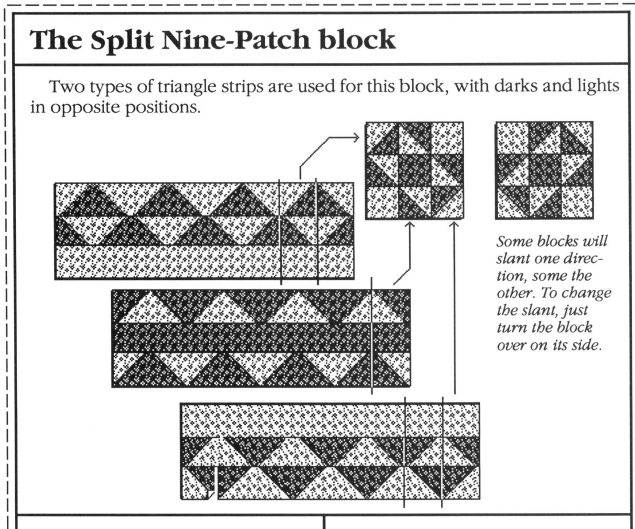

Some blocks will slant one direction, some the other. To change the slant, just turn the block over on its side.

If lights and darks are not where you need them, just cut off one triangle set and move the strip over a bit until darks and lights match the diagram. Sew the piece you cut off to the other end. (Sew it to the row above so it doesn't get lost, but don't sew it to the adjoining triangle. You'll cut there later.)

You can avoid this piecing by planning ahead. Make both types of strips in the first place. If making eight blocks or less, make two 4 x 4 checkerboards. Cut one through the light squares first, one through the dark first. For bigger

projects, make two 4 x 8 checkerboards. Cut one type of strip from one checkerboard, the other type from the other checkerboard.

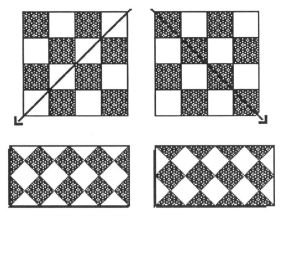

"Puzzle" patchwork

With this block (and Hovering Hawks, page 130), you might feel like you're putting a puzzle together. Some pieces just don't seem to fit anywhere! To avoid confusion, sort and stack the chains ahead of time.

It's worth the bother. Puzzle blocks can form such interesting new combinations when you assemble them into the quilt top. Have fun!

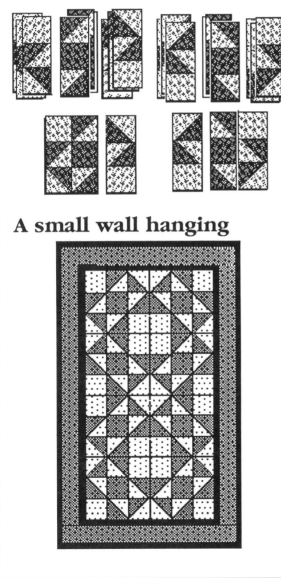

A small wall hanging

Color Plate 8 shows this project using eight Split Nine-Patch blocks.

To duplicate it, use 1/2 yd. of light fabric, 3/4 yd. of dark, 1/4 yd. of an accent color, and 2/3 yd. for backing. Make the blocks with 5" x 21" Alpha strips.

Combining Split Nine-Patch and regular Nine-Patch blocks

Here's how these two blocks might look together. Remember, you can make the Split Nine-Patch all slant the same direction by turning the blocks on their sides.

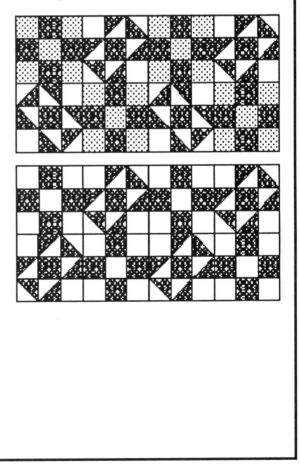

Split Nine-Patch wall hanging

While this looks like a combination of two blocks, it's actually 16 identical blocks with novelty sashing. The project is 36" square.

Fabric needed:

Dark: 1-1/4 yds.

Light: 5/8 yd.

Accent squares: 1/4 yd.

Border print: 1-1/8 yds.

Backing: 1-1/8 yds.

Batting: 38" square

No cutting layout is given; cut all strips cross-grain, except border fabric.

1. Cut Alpha strips 4" x 17", six light and six dark.

2. Make two 4 x 6 checkerboards.

3. Turn checkerboards on the bias; see page 39.

Cut one checkerboard through the **light** first. Cut strips like this:

Cut one checkerboard through the **dark** first. Cut strips like this:

4. Cut Beta strips (about 2-3/8" x 19"): four of light and two of dark.

5. Make six design panels. Cut cross sections and sort them.

6. Make 16 blocks. Measure them (they'll be about 5-3/4").

7. Make sashing with accent squares attached. Cut two strips of dark fabric, 4-1/4" x 31". Cut two strips of accent fabric, Beta width and the same length. Sew as shown on page 11. Measure width; trim dark side if necessary to match block width. Cut into 24 cross sections, Beta width. Use 12 strips (some turned one way, some the other) to join the blocks in rows of four as shown above. Join the other 12 strips with Beta-width squares (five light and four medium) to make long sashing.

8. Add inner border of same fabric, 4" wide.

9. Add final border of border fabric, any width. Miter corners.

10. Assemble backing, batting, and quilt top. Quilt and bind your favorite way.

Split Nine-Patch charts

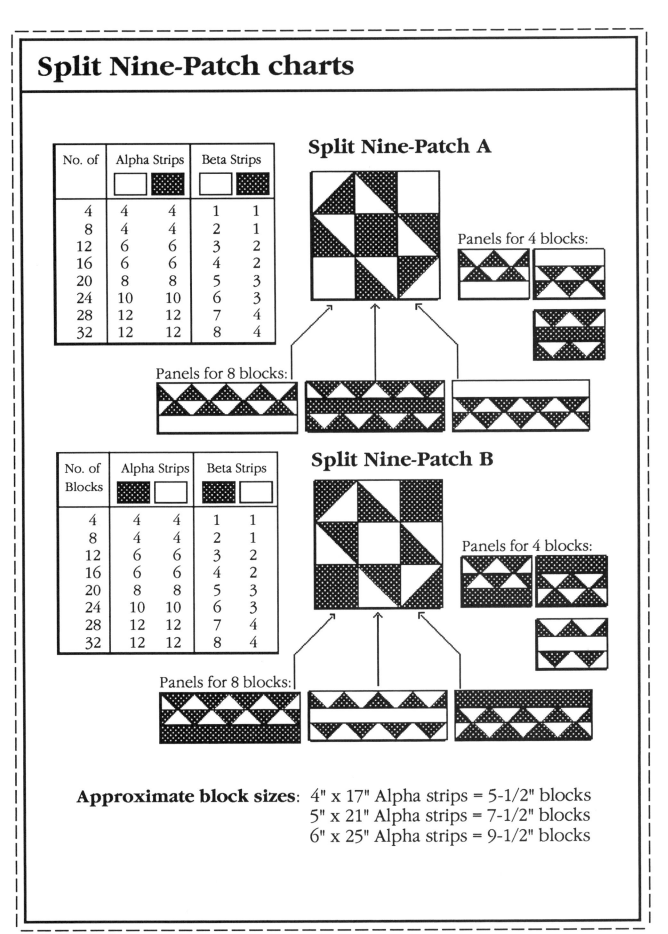

No. of	Alpha Strips		Beta Strips	
	☐	▨	☐	▨
4	4	4	1	1
8	4	4	2	1
12	6	6	3	2
16	6	6	4	2
20	8	8	5	3
24	10	10	6	3
28	12	12	7	4
32	12	12	8	4

Split Nine-Patch A

Panels for 4 blocks:

Panels for 8 blocks:

No. of Blocks	Alpha Strips		Beta Strips	
	▨	☐	▨	☐
4	4	4	1	1
8	4	4	2	1
12	6	6	3	2
16	6	6	4	2
20	8	8	5	3
24	10	10	6	3
28	12	12	7	4
32	12	12	8	4

Split Nine-Patch B

Panels for 4 blocks:

Panels for 8 blocks:

Approximate block sizes: 4" x 17" Alpha strips = 5-1/2" blocks
5" x 21" Alpha strips = 7-1/2" blocks
6" x 25" Alpha strips = 9-1/2" blocks

The Maple Leaf block

There are so many blocks you can put together with strips of triangles and Beta strips that it was hard to choose which ones to show you. Here's a quick look at Maple Leaf, which you can use plain or with an embroidered or appliquéd stem. Make up your own projects, using the chart on page 117.

Some projects have blocks with sashing on one side only.

Try this as a border on a large

The "leaves" disappear in the arrangement above (left). Even this block can be combined with Nine-Patch blocks, if the leaves have high contrast and the Nine-Patch low contrast (right).

Maple Leaf and Friendship Star charts

Maple Leaf

This is only one of many color combinations which are possible with this block.

No. of Blocks	Alpha Strips		Beta Strips		
4	2	2	1	1	1
8	2	2	2	2	1
12	4	4	3	3	2
16	4	4	4	4	2
20	6	6	5	5	3
24	6	6	6	6	3
28	8	8	7	7	4
32	8	8	8	8	4

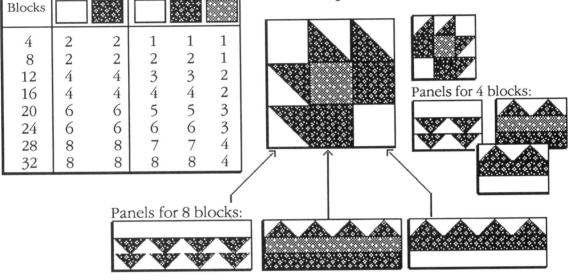

Panels for 4 blocks:

Panels for 8 blocks:

Friendship Star

*You'll make both types of blocks. Turning a star on its side does **not** change the direction it revolves.*

No. of Blocks	Alpha Strips		Beta Strips	
4	2	2	2	1
8	2	2	4	1
12	4	4	6	2
16	4	4	8	2
20	6	6	10	3
24	6	6	12	3
28	8	8	14	4
32	8	8	16	4

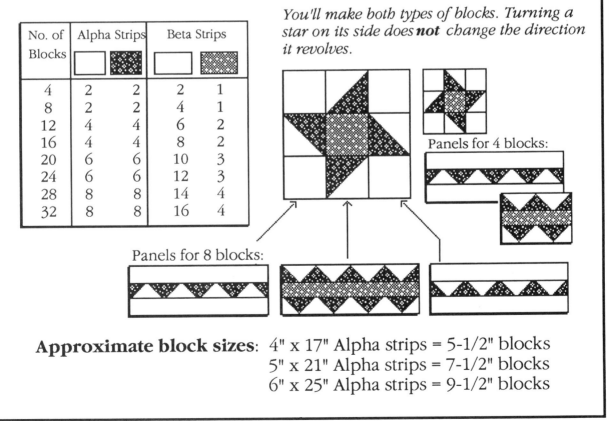

Panels for 4 blocks:

Panels for 8 blocks:

Approximate block sizes: 4" x 17" Alpha strips = 5-1/2" blocks
5" x 21" Alpha strips = 7-1/2" blocks
6" x 25" Alpha strips = 9-1/2" blocks

Irish Star quilt

This is a combination of 24 **Friendship Stars** and 25 **Nine-Patch B** blocks in an Irish Chain arrangement. Finished project is about 60" square. No cutting diagrams given; cut all strips cross-grain.

Fabric needed:

Dark A (for Stars) 1/2 yd.

Dark B (for Nine-Patch): 1 yd.

Light fabric: 2 yds.

Medium fabric: 1 yd.

Backing : 3-1/2 yds.

Batting: 62" square

One way to quilt this project is by machine:

Stitch diagonally this way, then stitch the other direction

Design ideas:

• **You might see the stars** or the **chains** or the **"balloons"** around the chains, depending on the colors used. To try out a design, sew up a 2 x 4 checkerboard and turn it on the bias. Cut out individual triangle sets, add squares the same size, and make test blocks to see how your colors will work. You don't need to sew them; you can just paste them up or lay them out.

• **For a more complicated design**, get 3/4 yd. of a second light fabric for the Nine-Patch blocks. (Decrease the first light fabric to 1-5/8 yds.)

• **Substitute Shoofly A or Snowball A** for the stars in this project, or substitute stars for the Shoofly or Snowball blocks in the projects on pages 108 or 109.

---

1. Cut Alpha strips. Spread out dark and light fabric and fold over. Cut three stacks of strips, 5" x 21" (six strips of Dark A and six of light fabric).

2. Make checkerboards, one 4 x 4 and one 4 x 8.

3. Turn on the bias. Cut one panel into strips like this:

Cut the other into strips like this:

Measure the strips of triangles (they'll be about 3-1/8" x 25").

4. Cut Beta width strips, selvage to selvage, 12 light and three medium. Trim to Beta length. Use leftover light pieces to help make the Nine-Patch blocks.

5. Make design panels for the stars; you'll need nine. (Use the chart on page 117.)

6. Cut chains and assemble 24 blocks. On your first blocks, pin everything first and double-check before sewing; it's easy to turn the triangles the wrong way accidentally. Half the stars will revolve one way, half the other.

7. Make panels for the Nine-Patch B blocks (see page 32). Cut **Dark B** fabric into 10 selvage-to-selvage strips, Beta width. Cut to match to the light strips left over in Step 4 and assemble panels. (They can be any length for Nine-Patch blocks.) Cut three or four more light strips to use with the rest of the dark strips.

8. Cut cross sections and assemble 25 blocks.

9. Assemble seven rows of seven blocks each, with stars revolving as shown.

10. Make borders. Cut remainder of **Dark B** fabric into five cross-grain strips, Beta width. Cut six strips 4" wide from the medium fabric (or just divide equally).

11. Assemble backing (use Number 2 on page 15).

12. Quilt and bind as you wish (see page 118).

Three-Patch sampler

This twin throw, about 54" x 70" is made of 24 blocks, four repeats of each of the five blocks presented so far in this chapter and four Nine-Patch blocks from Chapter 2. See Color Plate 3 for an example of this project.

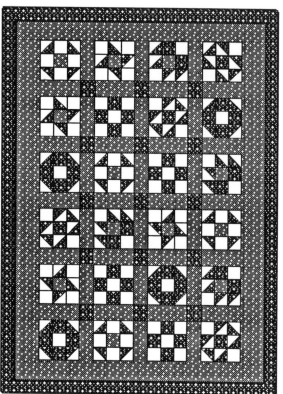

Fabric needed:

Dark: 1-3/4 yds.

Light: 1-1/4 yds.

Medium: 1-3/4 yds.

Backing: 3-1/4 yds.

Batting: 56" x 72"

For a larger project, add sawtooth border (Size 4 on page 98).

1. Cut Alpha strips, cross-grain, six light and six dark (5" x 21").

2. Make into checkerboards, one 4 x 4 and one 4 x 8.

3. Turn on the bias as usual. Mark centers in the small panel and cut it apart into bias strips. The large panel should be cut apart so darks and lights in the strips are in **opposite** positions from the four strips already cut, so determine which direction that will be. Mark it and cut bias strips from it.

4. Measure bias strips (they'll be about 3-1/8" x 25"). Cut Beta strips to match: **six of dark, ten of light, and two of medium**. Cut lengthwise to allow long strips for borders. Most of these Beta strips will be cut in two (about 3-1/8" x 12-1/2") to make the panels. Notice how the **dark** strips are cut: four long, then four half-strips to replace the other two long ones. By doing it this way, you can avoid cutting fabric needed for borders.

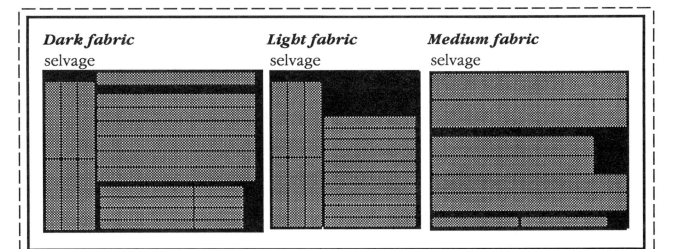

Dark fabric
selvage

Light fabric
selvage

Medium fabric
selvage

5. Sew together into design panels, following diagrams for four blocks in each case (Nine-Patch, page 32; Shoofly and Snowball, page 110; Split Nine-Patch, page 115; Maple Leaf and Friendship Star, page 117). You may want to do Friendship Star and Split Nine-Patch first to have first choice of strips.

6. Make blocks, referring if necessary to pages where blocks were originally introduced.

7. Make sashing and contrasting squares. Press and measure blocks (they'll be about 8-1/2"). Cut two strips that wide the full length of the **medium** fabric, 64". Cut one strip, 48" long and Beta width, lengthwise from the **dark** fabric. Sew it to one of the 8" strips, as shown on page 12. Cut that panel apart into Beta width

sections, making 15 sashing strips with dark squares attached. Fold and stack remaining strips for easy cutting and cut 23 more sashing strips, without squares.

8. Join blocks to make quilt top.

9. Make borders. Cut remaining medium fabric into four strips 5" wide. Trim to fit quilt top and sew in place making inner border. Cut six 4" strips from remaining dark fabric. Trim to fit and sew in place for outer border.

10. Make backing. (Use Number 1 on page 15).

11. Quilt and bind with your favorite method.

Medallion quilt

Little blocks don't need to be dull: 15 Snowball blocks, 24 Split Nine-Patch, and a sawtooth border make an exciting quilt, 60" x 75". See this project in Color Plate 13. This quilt looks complicated, but it's not. Make it elegant with rich colors and beautiful border prints. We'll use **one light fabric** throughout for unity, but **three or four dark fabrics** for variety. (It's easier to find rich, interesting **dark** fabrics than light ones.)

Fabric needed:

Light: 2-1/4 yds.

Dark A: 1/2 yd.

Dark B: 1-1/8 yds.

Dark C: 1/2 yd.

Dark border: 2/3 yd.

Border print: 2-1/4 yds.

Backing: 3-1/2 yds.

Batting: 62" x 78"

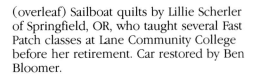

(overleaf) Sailboat quilts by Lillie Scherler of Springfield, OR, who taught several Fast Patch classes at Lane Community College before her retirement. Car restored by Ben Bloomer.

(right) Red Ohio Star, Variation A (see chart, page 86), by Lillie Scherler; white quilt by Marjorie France of Eugene, OR; pillow, Variation F, by Anita Hallock.

(below) Two Sister's Choice blocks combined with an appliqué block, by Nancy Parritt (a student of Nancy Congleton, who teaches at Brewer Fabrics in Brewer, ME).

(left) Ida Duncan of Eugene, OR, used a special step to keep all Sailboat blocks facing the same direction (see page 125). The boats were made with 4″ Alpha strips and set together with decorative sashing. The 48 Nine-Patch blocks at the intersections were strip-pieced, of course, but it was still an exacting and time-consuming task to line up seams on that many tiny blocks.

(below) Two gorgeous Christmas wall hangings made from one set of 13″ Sister's Choice blocks and two appliqué blocks, by Frances Faucher of Bangor, ME (a student of Nancy Congleton). Prairie points are added to the piece on the wall.

(right) Pine Tree wall hanging by Cathy Epperly, a partner at Creations Plus in Newark, DE. Tree trunk and background made from templates, but branches from a 4 × 4 checkerboard of 5″ Alpha strips. See Chapter 6.

Marilyn Ewing (student of Nancy Congleton) made this beautiful Christmas wall hanging, which doubles as a table runner—two blocks of Sister's Choice C are used with an appliqué block, all set on point. See page 140.

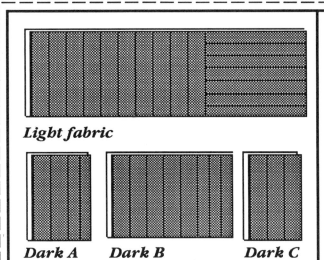

Light fabric

Dark A   **Dark B**   **Dark C**

(All fabric is shown doubled.)

Make checkerboards:

1. Cut all Alpha strips. Double-length strips work nicely for this project.

(a) Lay out the **light fabric** and **Dark A** with right sides together and three sides even. Fold over to make four layers. Trim ends and cut **two** 5" wide stacks. Just leave the strips full length for now (44").

(b) Spread **Dark B** out with the light fabric and cut **five** 5" stacks of strips.

(c) Spread out **Dark C** with the light fabric and cut **three** 5" stacks.

2. Make checkerboards, either **4 x 8, or 4 x 4 size.**

Make Snowball blocks:

3. Turn the checkerboard of Dark A on the bias. Mark centers and cut strips. Measure to find Beta size.

4. Cut Beta strips (about 3-1/8" x 25").

(a) From **light fabric cut 14 strips** (cut with the grain, because they won't fit the other way). Save six for the Split Nine-Patch blocks and use eight for the Snowball blocks.

(b) From **Dark A** cut **two Beta strips.**

5. Make **six Snowball A design panels** (see chart on page 110). Make **16 blocks.** Sew 15 of them together to make the center panel of the quilt.

Make Split Nine-Patch blocks:

6. Turn checkerboards from Dark B on bias. Mark and cut strips. Cut some though the dark and some through the light so you have both types.

7. Cut three Beta strips from Dark B. Make nine Split Nine-Patch design panels (see chart on page 115).

8. Make 24 Split Nine-Patch blocks. Sew into sets of six like this (switch directions in the center:)

9. Choose first border print to go around the Snowball panel. Lay the Split Nine-Patch sets out around the panel to see how much distance there is between the blocks. There will probably be about 3" or 3-1/2". **Add 1" for seam allowances** and choose border sections that width and with colors that complement both blocks. If the border you want to use isn't wide enough, add a narrow black border on one side to widen it. **Sew borders in place**, mitering corners.

10. **Sew Split Nine-Patch blocks** to sides, then to the top and bottom.

Make Sawtooth border and outer borders:

11. **Add a second border section.** If you make it Beta width, it should make the quilt just the right size for the sawtooth borders. (If you want wider borders, you can make the sawtooth border longer, and adjust this border as you did in Step 9, adding narrow black borders if needed.

12. **Turn Dark C checkerboards on the bias**, mark, and cut into strips.

13. **Make sawtooth borders** (see Chapter 6). Fit the border to the project as shown on pages 100-101, or do it like this: Sew **10 strips** together. Cut the remaining two strips in two and sew as shown (**14 rows** on that side). Cut chains and sew end to end, changing directions as shown on page 100. Sew chains to the quilt, keeping seams aligned with seams on the Split Nine-Patch blocks.

(**Note:** If you used extra-wide borders in Step 11, use **11 and 15 rows**. Make a 2 x 4 checkerboard for the extra triangles.)

14. **Add final border.** Use the fourth dark fabric or another border print.

15. **Make backing.** (Use Number 1 or 2 on page 15.)

16. **Quilt and bind** with your favorite method.

To vary this project:

Try **Friendship Star** blocks instead of Split Nine-Patch. Have stars revolving clockwise on one side, counterclockwise on the other side.

Step 1: Use only three double-long Alpha strips of Dark B and light fabric.

Step 4: Make 20 instead of 14 Beta strips of light fabric.

The Sailboat block

These last two blocks are on a grid of four squares each way. (I call them "Four-Patch" rather than "Sixteen-Patch," as I explained on page 105.)

First, the Sailboat. Two panels are used to make this block:

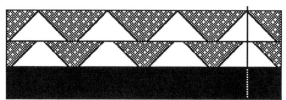

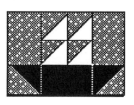

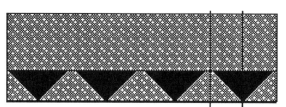

"Sky" strips are extra-wide. Usually the straight strips you join to the strips of triangles are **Beta** width (the width of the strips of triangles). If I were strict about that, I'd use two Beta strips to make the sky. But there's no sense having a seam where you don't need it, so leave the sky strips extra wide (twice Beta width, minus 1/2" for unneeded seam allowances). There's a special chart with these sizes included with the charts on page 129.

Water strips are optional. These are added last or are not used at all. Sometimes they double as sashing. They are Beta width and the length of the block.

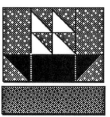

The direction of the sails can vary. Normally two types of boats are made at one time, half sailing east and half sailing west.

If you don't want both types, do this: Sew two strips of triangles together. Cut cross sections. Sew together pairs with the same slant. Just turn those slanting the wrong way on their sides. Add boat pieces separately.

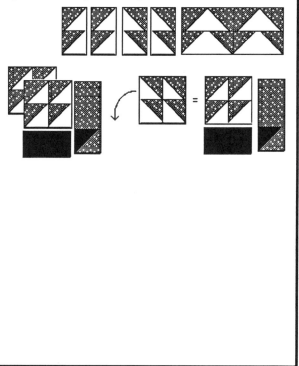

Two Sailboat quilts for bunk beds

Make 32 big blocks (12-1/2"). Combine 15 with boats sailing the same direction in each quilt; you'll have two extra blocks. Size will be about 52" x 90". For simplicity, I'm referring to the fabrics as blue, white, and red, because that's a favorite color scheme for this boat. You can use other colors, of course.

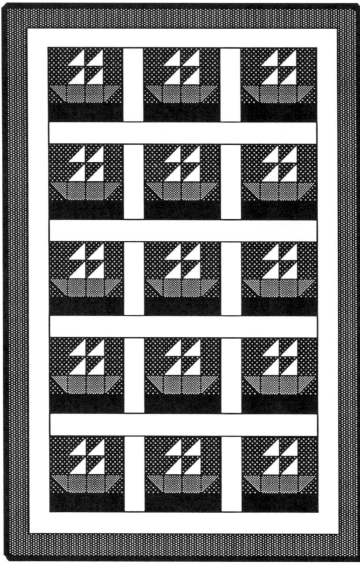

Note: *Want a wider quilt with sawtooth borders? See page 128.*

Yardage for both quilts:	Red: 1-1/2 yds.
Blue A (sky): 4-1/2 yds.	Blue B (water): 7/8 yd.
White: 4-1/2 yds.	Backing yardage: See page 128.

1. Cut Alpha strips, 6" x 25", **12 of Blue A, eight of white,** and **four of red.** Cut off two 32" sections of blue fabric and one 26" section of white fabric. Spread out four layers with ends and selvages even: First, **white,** right side up, then **blue**, right side down, then **blue,** right side up, then **red** on top, right side down.

(a) Cut **four** stacks of strips (with grain) through all layers. Remove the red.

(b) Cut **two more** stacks through the other three layers. Remove the blue (save these for sky strips).

(c) Cut **two more** white strips. There's room for only one here, so cut the other one from the big piece of white fabric, again parallel to selvage.

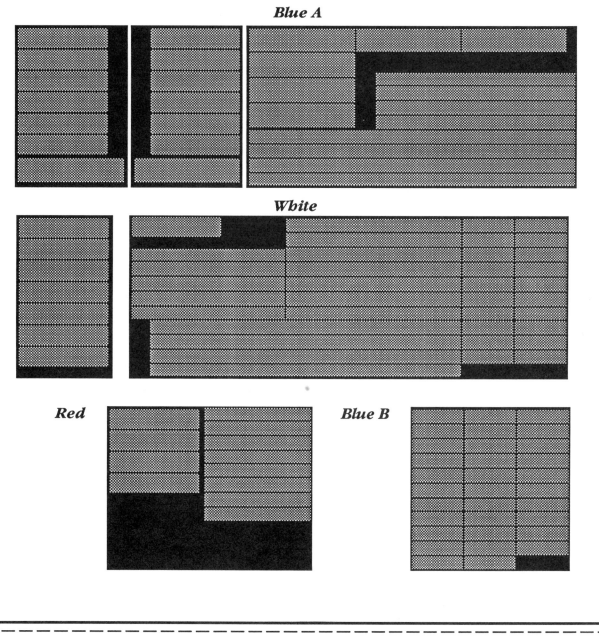

Blue A

White

Red

Blue B

2. Sew 4 x 8 checkerboards, two from blue and white, one from blue and red.

3. **Turn checkerboards on the bias** and mark centers (page 91).

4. Cut strips of triangles and measure them .

5. Make design panels. Cut eight Beta strips (about 3-3/4" x 30") from red fabric to make the boats. Cut eight sky strips from Blue A (7" x 30"). Make panels as shown on page 125, eight of each type.

6. Make blocks. Add **water strips** cut from Blue B (Beta width and the length of the blocks, about 13").

7. Make sashing. Cut white fabric into Beta-width strips. Trim as needed:

(a) **Cut 20 strips** the length of the blocks. Sew blocks into rows of three boats.

(b) **Cut 12 strips** for long sashing and top and bottom borders (about 45"). Join all rows to make two quilt tops.

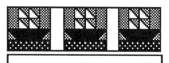

(c) **Cut four borders** to fit sides.

8. Add outer borders from blue fabric. Illustration shows 4" borders, but you can make them a little skimpy and use much less backing fabric.

9. Make backing: Skimpy (about 52" x 87"): Use six yards. Make as shown on Number 1 on page 15. **Larger** (about 58" x 90"): Get 7-2/3 yds. Divide into three equal sections (about 92"). Divide one section in two lengthwise (22" x 92"). Use one large section and one half section for each quilt.

10. Quilt and bind with your favorite methods. Use durable fabric.

Wider version of Sailboat quilts

Add a sawtooth border and extra blue border on each side to make quilts about 66" x 90". Needs an extra 1-1/2 yds. blue and 3/4 yd. white.

After Step 7, make sawtooth borders. See Chapter 6. Cut seven blue and seven white strips, 6" x 25", and make a 4 x 8 and a 4 x 6 checkerboard. Use 13 strips of triangles. When you make one long panel, don't change directions; keep all triangles facing the same way.

Wider version, Step 8. Sew first blue border to **sides only.** Cut sawtooth chains and sew in place. Add top and bottom blue borders and another 3" side border.

Wider version, Step 9. Make backing, using 9-3/4 yds.

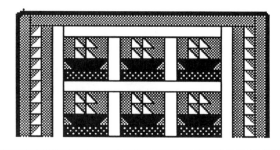

Sailboat block charts

Sailboat A

Half the blocks normally face one way, half the other. (See page 125.)

No. of Blocks	Alpha Strips			Sky	Boat	Water
4	2	4	2	1	1	4
8	2	4	2	2	2	8
12	4	6	2	3	3	12
16	4	6	2	4	4	16
20	6	10	4	5	5	20
24	6	10	4	6	6	24
28	8	12	4	7	7	28
32	8	12	4	8	8	32

See the chart below for strip sizes.

This variation is used in Color Plate 21.

Panels for 4 blocks:

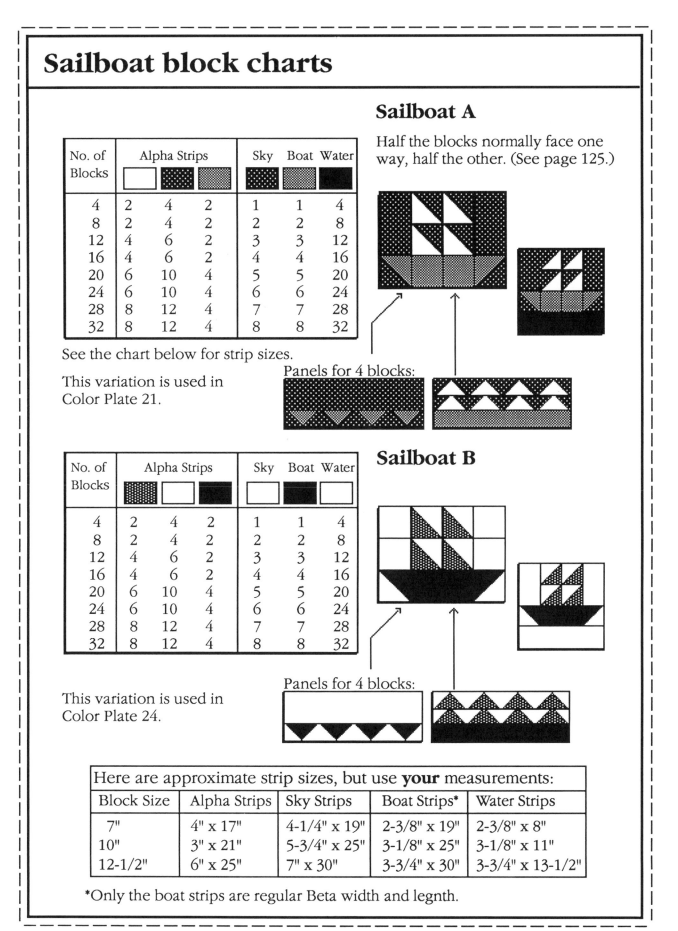

Sailboat B

No. of Blocks	Alpha Strips			Sky	Boat	Water
4	2	4	2	1	1	4
8	2	4	2	2	2	8
12	4	6	2	3	3	12
16	4	6	2	4	4	16
20	6	10	4	5	5	20
24	6	10	4	6	6	24
28	8	12	4	7	7	28
32	8	12	4	8	8	32

This variation is used in Color Plate 24.

Panels for 4 blocks:

Here are approximate strip sizes, but use **your** measurements:

Block Size	Alpha Strips	Sky Strips	Boat Strips*	Water Strips
7"	4" x 17"	4-1/4" x 19"	2-3/8" x 19"	2-3/8" x 8"
10"	3" x 21"	5-3/4" x 25"	3-1/8" x 25"	3-1/8" x 11"
12-1/2"	6" x 25"	7" x 30"	3-3/4" x 30"	3-3/4" x 13-1/2"

*Only the boat strips are regular Beta width and legnth.

The Hovering Hawks block

This block is similar to the Split Nine-Patch; it's a "puzzle" block. You'll swear sometimes that pieces won't fit anywhere, but they will. Make two types of blocks with the design slanting different directions. If you turn blocks on their sides, they'll slant the other direction.

Projects which are easiest to calculate are those with four strips of triangles in each set, since a 4 x 4 checkerboard makes four strips. This one has five, and one's an oddball. Where do you get the extra strip of triangles?

In the project below, you borrow it from the panel for the

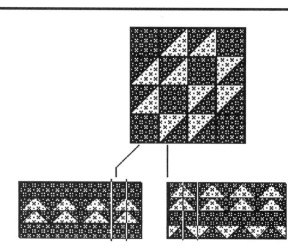

sawtooth border. When planning your own projects with the charts on page 132, you'll make an extra 4 x 4 checkerboard (which you'll cut apart in the opposite direction from the others).

Hovering Hawks wall hanging

This project has four small blocks and a sawtooth border. It is about 24" square. An example of this is shown on the front cover.

Fabric needed:

Light (including backing): 1 yd.

Dark: 1 yd.

Batting: 26" square

1. Cut Alpha strips. Spread out light and dark fabric with right sides together and fold like this: Cut three stacks 4" x 17", leaving a large area of **light** fabric for the backing. This makes **six light** and **six dark** strips.

selvage

2. Sew checkerboards, one 4 x 4 and one 4 x 8.

3. Turn the smaller checkerboard on the bias. Mark the centers.

4. Cut strips of triangles and measure them.

5. Cut three Beta strips (about 2-3/8" x 19") of **dark** fabric and mark them.

6. Make panels like this:

7. Turn the larger checkerboard on the bias. Mark it (decide which direction; you need to cut strips with darks and lights in the opposite position from the ones already in the panel). Cut only one strip off now, and sew it at the arrow.

8. Cut panels into chains and find chains that go together. (Some chains must be reversed. Some fit blocks that slant one direction; others fit in blocks that slant the opposite direction.) **Make four blocks.**

9. Sew blocks together. Measure design. (It'll be about 12".)

10. Add first border. Cut strips of dark fabric, Beta width. Sew them on.

11. Make sawtooth borders. Cut large panel into strips of triangles. Sew **five strips** and one

half strip together. Make chains and fit to project as shown in Chapter 6.

12. Make outer borders, 2" wide or wider, from dark fabric. Sew them in place. Press and measure to determine backing size.

13. Cut backing from the **light fabric.** Fit backing, batting and design to each other. **Quilt and bind** with your favorite methods.

Hovering Hawks variations

● **Omit the Sawtooth border.** Make a 2 x 4 checkerboard instead of a 4 x 8 for the extra strip (actually two half-strips) for Step 7.

● **Add more color.** Make the inner Beta strip and the border from a new fabric, as shown here. For an example of this variation, see Color Plate 8.

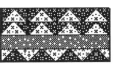

● **Change the block arrangement.** Sew the blocks together so lines radiate from the center like this:

See Color Plate 12 for an example.

Hovering Hawks charts

Hovering Hawks A

You'll make two types of blocks. (They slant the other way if you turn them on their sides.)

No. of Blocks	Alpha Strips		Beta Strips
4	4	4	3
8	6	6	6
12	8	8	9
16	10	10	12
20	14	14	15
24	16	16	18
28	18	18	21
32	20	20	24

You'll need to piece an occasional strip to make the darks and lights and zigs and zags work out right. See page 112.

Hovering Hawks B

No. of Blocks	Alpha Strips		Beta Strips
4	4	4	3
8	6	6	6
12	8	8	9
16	10	10	12
20	14	14	15
24	16	16	18
28	18	18	21
32	20	20	24

Approximate block size: 4" x 17" Alpha strips =   7-1/2" blocks
5" x 21" Alpha strips = 10-1/2" blocks
6" x 25" Alpha strips = 12-1/2" blocks

Planning sheets for blocks in Chapter 7

Use these diagrams to plan your color scheme and do calculations. Make photocopies of this page or page 134. Cut out the diagrams for your block and color with colored pencils to represent your fabrics. See pages 174-175 for aids in calculating yardage. Clip these small diagrams to a large piece of paper where you do your calculations, or tape them to your sewing machine to refer to as you sew.

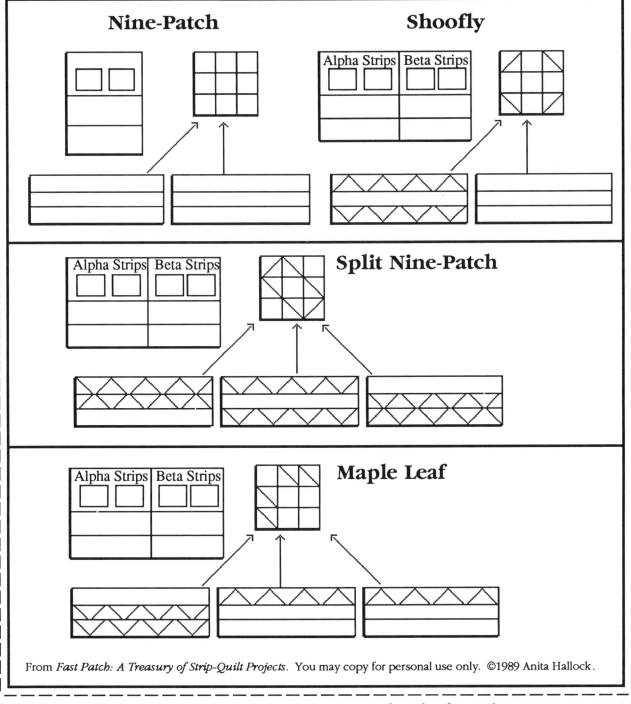

There are many other blocks which could be made with these same techniques. As you get more confident, use grid paper to plan new blocks.

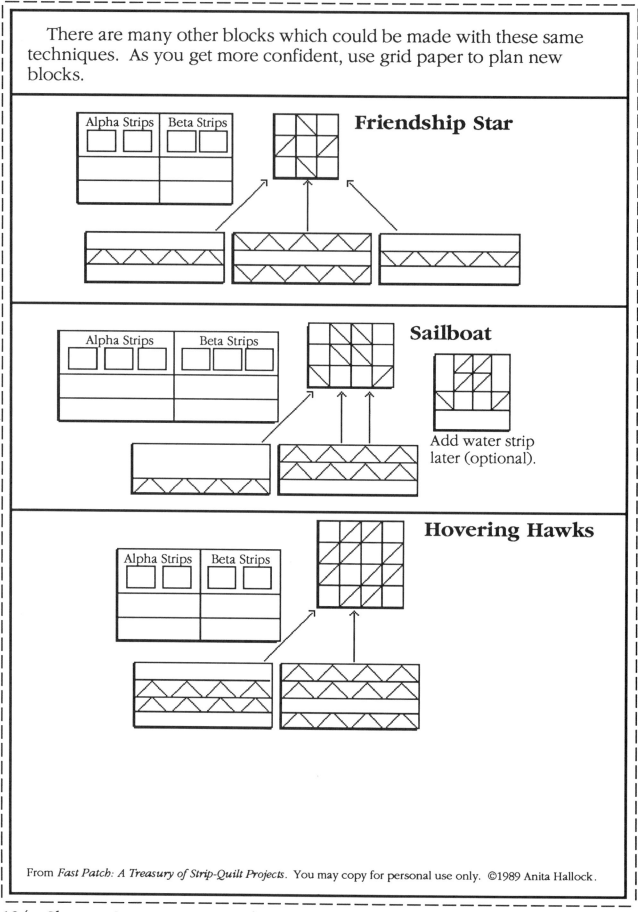

Friendship Star

Alpha Strips   Beta Strips

Sailboat

Alpha Strips   Beta Strips

Add water strip later (optional).

Hovering Hawks

Alpha Strips   Beta Strips

8.   *Five-Patch Favorites*

These blocks are on a grid of five squares in each direction. There are so many wonderful blocks in this category, it was hard to choose which ones to include. These blocks are not for beginners. Before attempting Five-Patch blocks, you should be comfortable with the rotary cutter, should be able to turn a checkerboard on the bias without thinking twice, should know your personal size for Beta strips, and should find it easy to follow the craftsmanship rules on pages 49-50. As usual, triangle strips are made from checkerboards, and match-ing Beta strips make the squares.

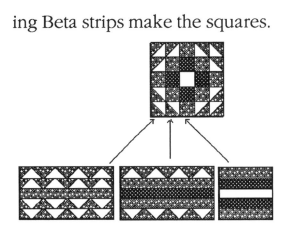

Blocks are made in sets of four, from three design panels—two full size and one half-size. Each block uses two chains from the larger panels, but only one (for the center) from the smaller panel.

Double Irish Chain

The Double Irish Chain is a very popular Five-Patch block that uses only squares. Try it first, if you aren't too sure about bias panels, Beta strips, and so on.

There are actually two blocks, a patchwork block and a connecting block. (I'll call it a "plain" block on the chart.)

Strips don't need to be any special length this time since they don't match strips of triangles. They can even be a full 44" long.

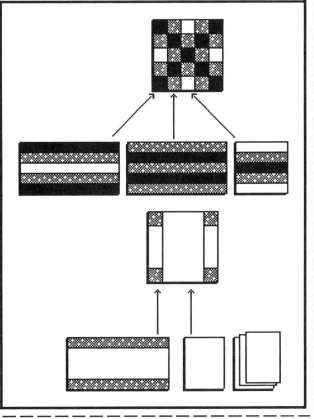

Double Irish Chain crib quilt

Finished size is about 38" x 58".

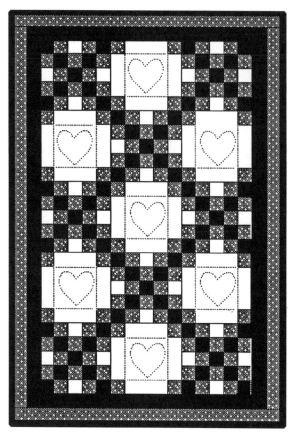

Fabric needed:

Dark: 2/3 yd.

Medium: 1 yd.

Light: 1 yd.

Backing: 1-3/4 yds.

Batting: 40" x 60"

All strips are cut cross-grain. No cutting diagrams are given.

1. Cut 2-1/2" x 44" strips: five dark, eight medium, two light.

2. Make pieced blocks. Sew into panels as shown on page 135, cutting one strip of each color in half. (Some strips won't be used yet.) Cut 2-1/2" cross sections. Make eight blocks.

3. Make plain blocks: Cut one strip of light fabric, 6-1/2" x 44", and sew a medium strip to each side of it, checking to make sure seams will line up with those in the pieced blocks. Cut 14 cross sections, 2-1/2" wide. Cut seven pieces of light fabric, 6-1/2" x 11", for the center. Assemble blocks.

4. Join all blocks. Press and measure quilt top.

5. Cut borders, 2-1/2" wide or wider, from dark and medium fabrics. Piece to fit.

6. Quilt and bind with your favorite techniques.

Double Irish Chain chart

Here's a very handy chart with calculations for five popular Double Irish Chain arrangements. These arrangements are based on **10"-square, three-color** blocks made from **2-1/2" strips.** Borders can be 2-1/2" to 3"; increase them to 3-1/2" on the largest project.

On three projects I have you remove strips parallel to the selvage first. Make the **dark** and **medium** strips into borders. Cut some of the 6-1/2" x 11" pieces for the plain blocks from the **light** strips.

Strips for blocks are cut cross-grain. Some will be cut in half for the small panels.

To make a quilt this size (before quilting):		Buy this much fabric:	Remove (along selvage):	Cut 2-1/2" strips:			6-1/2" strips	6-1/2" x 11" pieces	Backing (see page 15):
8 pieced 7 plain 38" x 58"		■ 2/3 yd ▨ 1 yd □ 1 yd	None None None	5	8	2	1	7	1-3/4 yd (one piece)
				(These strips are all 44" long.)					
12 pieced 13 plain 58" square		■ 1 yd ▨ 1-1/2 yd □ 1-1/2 yd	None None None	7	12	4	2	13	3-2/3 yd (quilt type 2)
				(These strips are all 44" long.)					
18 pieced 17 plain 58" x 78"		■ 2-1/4 yd ▨ 2-1/3 yd □ 1-3/4 yd	12" 12" 11"	14	24	6	3	17	3-2/3 yd (quilt type 2)
				(These strips are all 32" long.)					
24 pieced 25 plain 78" x 78"		■ 2-1/2 yd ▨ 3 yd □ 2-1/3 yd	12" 12" 11"	20	33	8	4	25	5 yd (quilt type 4)
				(These strips are all 32" long.)					
32 pieced 31 plain 80" x 100"		■ 2-3/4 yd ▨ 3-1/2 yd □ 3 yd	14" 14" 11"	30	48	12	6	31	6 yd (quilt type 5)
				(These strips are all 30" long.)					

Panels and strips used for Sister's Choice block

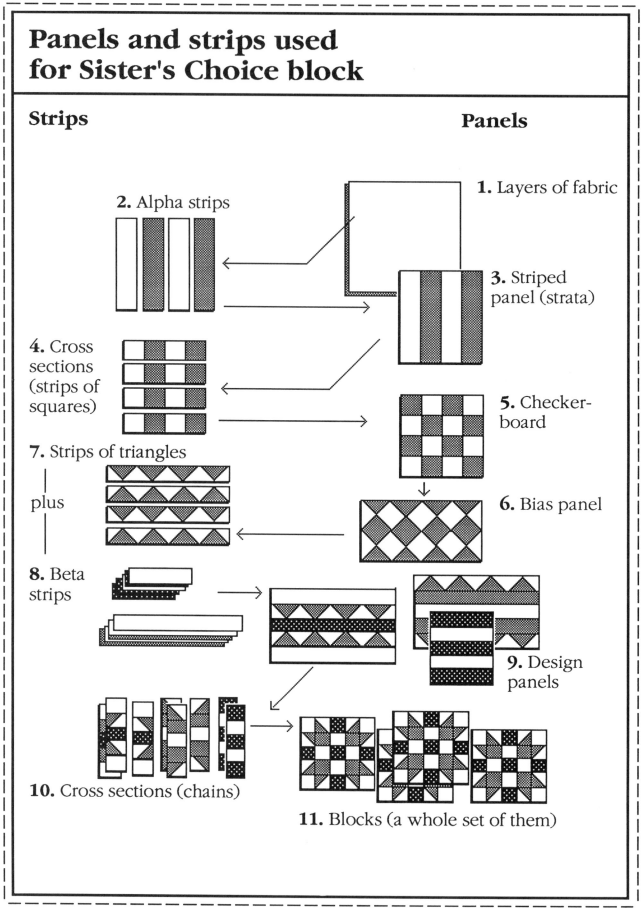

Strips

Panels

1. Layers of fabric

2. Alpha strips

3. Striped panel (strata)

4. Cross sections (strips of squares)

5. Checker-board

7. Strips of triangles

plus

6. Bias panel

8. Beta strips

9. Design panels

10. Cross sections (chains)

11. Blocks (a whole set of them)

A review of some basic ideas

Now back to the special Fast Patch blocks with triangles as well as squares.

This chapter is for advanced strip quilters. It gives lots of new blocks so you can calculate your own projects, and it only presents a few projects already worked up. Please review these special topics if you need to:

• Chapter 1 for basic quiltmaking and charts for sashing, backing, and binding.

• Page 17 for tips on making checkerboards.

• Page 33 for why we turn checkerboards on the bias.

• Pages 34-38 for how to turn various sizes of checkerboards on the bias.

• Page 42 for ideas about turning a whole quilt top on the bias.

• Page 48 for an explanation of terms like Alpha strips and design panels.

• Pages 49-50 for special rules for working with bias strips and design panels.

• Page 91 for how to mark centers of triangles for accurate alignment.

• Page 102 for a definition of Beta strips.

• Page 104 for how to mark Beta strips for accurate alignment with triangle strips.

Alpha Strips	Beta Strips	Final Piece	Block Size
Strips which make triangles (four times as long as they are wide, plus 1")	Strips which make squares (eight times as long as they are wide; match triangle strips)		(all Five-Patch except Double Irish Chain)
4" x 17"	**2-1/2" x 20"** or 2-3/8" x 19"* or 2-1/4" x 18"	**2"**(scant) or 1-7/8* or 1-3/4"	**9-1/2"†** 9"* 8-3/4"
5" x 21"	**3-1/4" x 26"** or 3-1/8" x 25"* or 3" x 24"	**2-5/8"** or 2-1/2"* or 2-3/8"	**13"** or 12-1/2"* or 12"
6" x 25"	**3-3/4" x 30"** or 3-5/8" x 29"* or 3-1/2" x 28"	**3-1/8"** or 3 "* or 2-7/8"	**15-1/2"** or 15"* or 14-1/2"

Size I see most often.

† *These should turn out the same as the Double Irish Chain with 2-1/2" strips, shouldn't they? But blocks with triangles seem to shrink up more than blocks with just squares.*

The Sister's Choice block

Sister's Choice is most people's favorite Five-Patch block because it's a pretty block and it's the easiest one to make with triangles. You'll see a lot of examples of this block in the color photo section.

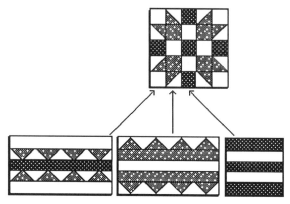

This panel is for centers.

My charts and layouts always call for full Beta strips, but you'll cut some strips in half. If you're only making four blocks, there'll be a **half strip left over** (whatever color is in the very center of the block). When you're making dozens of blocks, make these panels full length too, if you wish, but make only half as many of them as you do the other two.

First try a set of four blocks. These blocks will be made with 5" Alpha strips and will be about 12-1/2" square. (You can substitute 4" Alpha strips and make 9" blocks, if that doesn't confuse you.)

Fabric needed for 4 blocks:

Medum fabric: 1/2 yd.

Light fabric: 5/8 yd.

Dark fabric: 1/3 yd.

1. **Cut Alpha strips.** Spread out light and medium fabrics, right sides together. Fold over to make four layers and cut one stack of strips 5" x 21" (two light and two medium).

2. **Make a 4 x 4 checkerboard. Turn it on the bias** (it doesn't matter which direction you cut first). Marking is optional; it's more accurate if you do.

3. **Cut strips and measure them.** They'll be about 3-1/8" x 25"; that's your Beta size.

4. **Cut Beta strips:** four light, three dark, two medium.

5. **Make design panels** that match the diagrams.

6. **Cut cross sections and assemble blocks.**

Some ideas for using your blocks

Combine them with appliqué blocks for wall hangings.

The beautiful projects in Color Plates 23, 25, and 27 each use two Sister's Choice blocks from 5" Alpha strips and one appliqué block. If you don't do appliqué, use a pretty printed panel or trade two blocks for an appliqué block done by a friend. (Your conscience may bother you because these blocks are so much easier than the appliqué blocks, but they're pretty enough to please anyone.)

Make this four-block wall hanging.

If you made the blocks with 4" Alpha strips, use them in this 24" square wall hanging. Cut Alpha and Beta strips cross-grain, borders lengthwise.

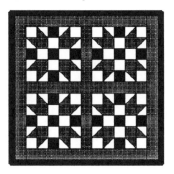

Fabric needed:

Medium: 1 yd. (includes backing and borders)

Light: 1/2 yd.

Dark: 3/8 yd. (includes binding)

Make four pillows.

Keep one or two for yourself and use the others for gifts or bazaars. You'll need an additional 1-1/2 yds. of fabric for borders and backing. Blocks from 5" Alpha strips will be about 16-18" with borders. Cut 16 strips of medium fabric 3" x 18" (four borders for each pillow), reserving large pieces for backing.

Use the blocks for a large quilt.

Calculations are given on page 142 for the quilt in Color Plate 20. Your practice block is Sister's Choice C; the one on the bed is slightly different. Here's how to adjust the instructions to your blocks: Your **light** and **medium** are the same as the "white" and "rose" in that project; get the amount called for. Get 2-1/4 yds. more of your **dark** fabric to replace the "green" and part of the "beige." "Beige" will be used only for sashing and inner border now; get 2-2/3 yds. of it. (You can substitute any colors, of course.)

You'll need 28 more blocks. See the chart on page 159 and cut the number of Alpha and Beta strips called for.

Queen-size Sister's Choice quilt

This is a queen-size quilt, about 95" x 105" before quilting. It uses thirty 12-1/2" blocks. (Make 32 blocks; use two for pillows.) You can substitute other colors.

Fabric needed to match the quilt in Color Plate 20

Rose: 3-3/8 yds.

White: 3 yds.

Beige: 3-1/3 yds.

Green: 1-1/2 yds.

Backing : 8-1/3 yds.

Batting: 96" x 108"

1. Cut Alpha strips. For easy handling cut off 42" sections of **white and rose** fabrics and use them for this step. Spread them out, right sides together, and fold over. Cut eight 5" stacks crossgrain. Just leave them full length, 44" long, or at least 33". (Eight double-length strips equals 16 regular-length strips given on the charts.)

selvage

2. Make into 4 x 8 checkerboards. Turn at least one of them on the bias and find the Beta size. It will be about 3-1/8" x 25".

3. Divide remaining rose fabric in two lengthwise pieces and set one aside to make the binding later.

4. Remove a 14" strip lengthwise from **beige** fabric for sashing.

5. Cut all the rest of the fabric into Beta-width lengthwise strips (except backing, of course). Cut carefully so you can get 13 lengthwise strips from the 44" fabric. Stack and fold the fabrics in whatever way suits your space, and cut through as many layers as you can handle.

Accuracy is important, so take your time. If some green or beige strips turn out a bit too narrow, use them for the **borders.**

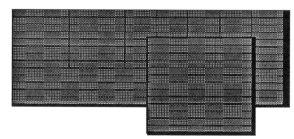

If you think this is a lot of cutting, remember you're making 564 little squares, dozens of sashing strips, and lots of borders. Thank goodness for rotary cutters!

6. Trim some strips to Beta length (about 25"—but use your measurement). You need **16 rose**, **four green**, and **16 beige strips** (leave four long strips intact for borders). You also need **32 white,** but you can probably cut only 26. Cut **12 half-length** strips to equal the other six and use them for the center panels.

7. Make design panels, eight of each.

8. Make blocks. You'll have enough to make 32 , but you need only 30. Discard less accurate sections if you wish.

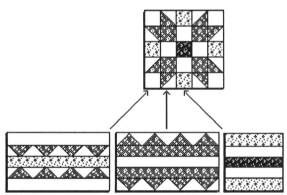

Review accuracy tips on page 50.

9. Cut 24 short sashing strips of beige to match the blocks (about 13" to 13-1/2"). Sew blocks together in rows of five blocks each.

10. Make a design decision now. Do you want solid sashing between the rows, or contrasting squares, as the example shows? There's no substitute for laying out the quilt on the floor and seeing which looks best. Use the long beige strips and some squares of green fabric (and other colors,

too—you might as well have the absolutely prettiest effect possible). Contrasting squares require more work but are usually well worth it.

11. For plain strips: Cut the 14" piece of beige fabric set aside earlier into Beta width strips also. Cut five strips to match the sets of five blocks (about 72" to 75"; use your measurement) and join the blocks into the quilt top.

  For contrasting squares: Sew contrasting strips, Beta width and a total of 65"-70" long, to one side of the beige strip (see page 12). Cut into 20 cross sections. Join them and plain strips to make five long sashing strips. Sew rows together.

12. Add borders. Use beige first, then an outer border of green (pieced).

13. Quilt and bind project with your favorite methods. Use the rose fabric set aside in Step 3 to make binding.

Sampler quilts

A beautiful sampler quilt is truly a pleasure to behold. You look at it again and again, each time deciding on your very favorite block. (You even appreciate the plainer blocks because they simplify your decision.) It's like a whole art exhibit instead of a single painting.

But a sampler is not automatically beautiful, especially if it's made by a group. A quilt should always be pretty; having a message is optional. A mixture of sentimental messages, photographs, and children's art might make a very nice scrapbook but a very ugly quilt (with a lot more work).

I was an art teacher for many years and have strong feelings about samplers. Visualize an art exhibit with each painting framed and spotlighted; then think of a bulletin board with paintings by artists with totally different styles crammed up next to each other. What a diffference! It is so sad to see some delicate masterpiece block sewn to a block with 5" squares of totally different colors. I would never contribute to a group quilt if there were no color restrictions and no guarantee that blocks would be put together thoughtfully.

Here are my personal "rules" for samplers:

1. Coordinate blocks; don't just have a hodgepodge. All of these Five-Patch blocks are already coordinated in size, scale, and mood.

2. Have some key colors used in all blocks.

3. Have each block framed by sashing in a color which complements all blocks. Have **dark/light contrast** between sashing and blocks, especially at the very **corners** of the blocks.

4. The final arrangement must be **balanced** by:

• **Colors.** For example, don't have all the **red** fabrics on the same side.

• **Values** (dark and light). Don't make one side "heavier" than the other.

• **Block types.** Alternate busy blocks like Pinwheels with quiet ones. Alternate blocks that radiate from the center, like Sister's Choice, with those which circle the center, like Crown of Thorns.

Making blocks for sampler quilts

Fast Patch is mainly an assembly-line method for making many blocks all the same. But here are some approaches you can follow to make samplers:

1. Make lots of four-block sets and make a **modified sampler,** with four repeats of each block (see Color Plate 14). If you're a production quiltmaker or have lots of grandchildren you've made promises to, make four different quilts.

2. Coordinate your work with three friends. Each of you makes six sets of four blocks. Mix blocks up so each person has 24 different blocks to work with.

3. Make single blocks, using the diagrams with the charts on pages 158-169. See Color Plates 19 and 15 for small quilts made that way. Use **2 x 4 checkerboards** or strips of triangles left over from other projects. See diagrams below.

4. Make single blocks with the "quarters and bars" approach. I'll introduce that method with the next project.

Here's how a 2 x 4 checkerboard would be converted into one **Crown of Thorns** *block. (See the pillow in Color Plate 1.)*

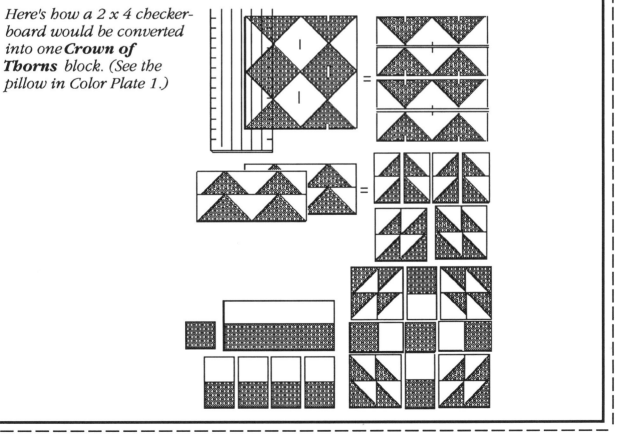

Fool's Square/Pinwheel blocks

Use these blocks for a sampler or make four pillows (matching or different). There's often more than one way to get the same effect, as you'll see in this project.

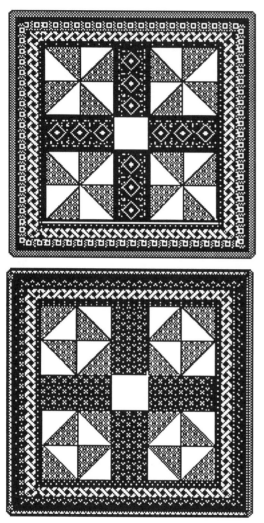

Pinwheel is the block on top. *Fool's Square* is shown below.

Fabric for blocks only:

Light fabric: 1/3 yd.

Medium fabric: 1/3 yd.

Dark fabric: 1/4 yd.

For four pillows, add:

Backing: 1 yd.

Border fabric with four repeats: 2 yds. (or 1 yd. if it has **two** border designs you like)

---

1. Cut Alpha strips. Lay out **light** and **medium** fabric with right sides together. Fold over and **cut 2 stacks of 5" x 21" strips** (four light, four dark).

2. Make two 4 x 4 checker-boards.

3. Turn checkerboards on the bias, cutting through the **light** first on one, through the **dark** first on the other. You don't need to mark centers this time.

4. Cut strips of triangles and measure to find Beta size (about 3-1/8" x 25").

5. Join all strips into pairs like this, matching points accurately.

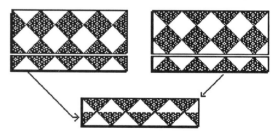

Now read to the end of this project. There are four ways to finish it. Each way begins at Step 6. Plus the Pinwheel block has a surprise twist to it, so be prepared.

Some ways to finish these blocks

Quarters and bars (A)

You could think of Five-Patch blocks as being made of four Two-Patch blocks or **"quarters,"** four **"bars,"** and a **center.**

6. Cut cross sections like this and measure them:

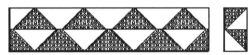

7. Cut 16 pieces that size (about 3-1/8" x 6") from **dark** fabric and **four light squares** the same width. (If you cut bars from **border fabric,** have each show the same section of the design.)

8. Sew the patchwork pieces together into quarters:

Make four quarters like this for each Pinwheel block you want. (Read ahead first.)

Make four quarters like this for each Fool's Square block you want.

9. Assemble blocks. Join four quarters, four bars, and a center to make each block.

Note: *Oops! That one quarter looked fine at first, but it really doesn't fit. Turn it over—it still doesn't fit. Some strange things can happen with the Pinwheel block. (Of course, they haven't happened to **you** yet because you're reading ahead, right?)*

*If you make **all** Pinwheel blocks, you'll find that half of the quarters revolve in one direction, half in the other. If you're saving pieces for Fool's Square, pick out pieces for Pinwheels **first** and make all quarters revolve in whichever direction you want. See Group 15 on page 152 for some of the possibilities. Pin everything together before you sew.*

When you finish, use the blocks for pillows (see Color Plate 1) or sampler quilts.

Quarters and bars (B)

6. Make quarters as before, Fool's Square and/or Pinwheel.

7. Make two-tone bars by strip-piecing. Two Beta strips make enough bars for two blocks.

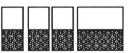

8. Assemble blocks.

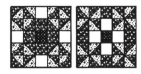

Modified design panels

6. Make quarters as before, Fool's Square or Pinwheels.

7. Cut only eight small bars. Attach to quarters like this:

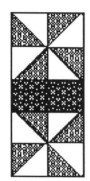

8. Make a panel. Cut two pieces of **dark** fabric 6" wide and half of a Beta length (about 12-1/2"). Cut one piece of **light** fabric, Beta width and half Beta length (about 3-1/8" x 12-1/2"). Sew them together like this and cut cross sections. Then assemble blocks.

(Look at the charts for Handy Andy, page 164, and Jack in the Box, page 169. This is the way you would make centers for those blocks to avoid those unnecessary seams.)

Design panels

6. Leave the strips intact instead of cutting cross sections.

7. Cut Beta strips, two of light and two of medium. Cut one of each in half and cut another half strip of dark.

8. Make design panels as shown here or in the slightly different combination shown on page 167.

9. Assemble blocks. Even with design panels, these blocks are special because you can make two different blocks from the same panels.

Design groups for "Quarters and Bars" samplers

Here are some common two-strip combinations and the type of quarters made from those strips. You usually make two different panels, and then choose any two blocks in that group. In some cases, you can make a single block from a single panel.

Add four bars and one center square to make each block. Solid-color bars are described on page 147. Two-tone bars made with strip techniques are shown on page 148.

I think it helps to decide on the color of sashing ahead of time. Then watch the corner color in each block. Pick a block with corners which contrast in each case.

Group 1

Group 2

Group 3

Group 4

Make only one pair of strips to make any single block in this group.

*Asterisks indicate the blocks used for the 20-block sampler on page 153.

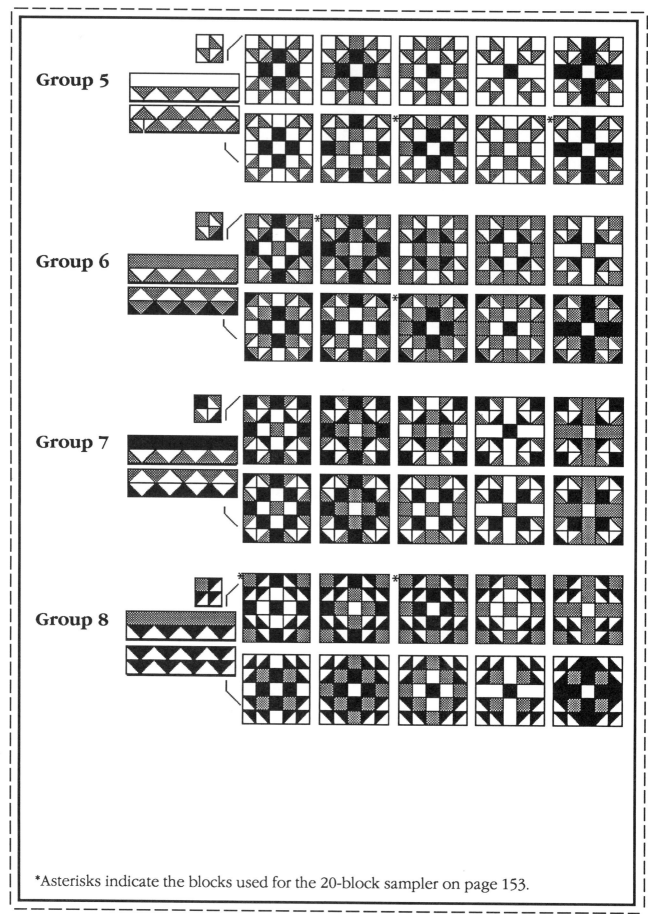

Group 5

Group 6

Group 7

Group 8

*Asterisks indicate the blocks used for the 20-block sampler on page 153.

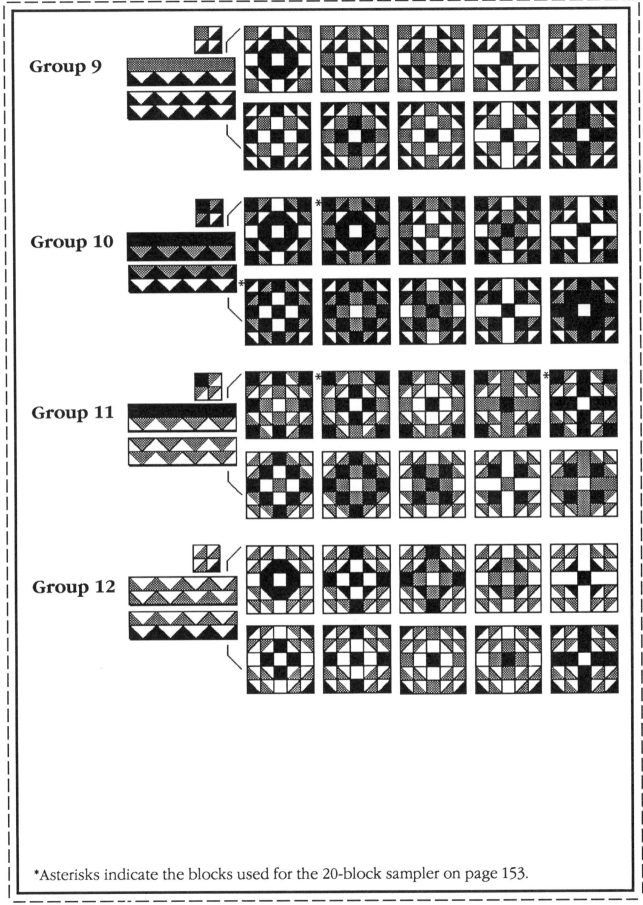

Group 9

Group 10

Group 11

Group 12

*Asterisks indicate the blocks used for the 20-block sampler on page 153.

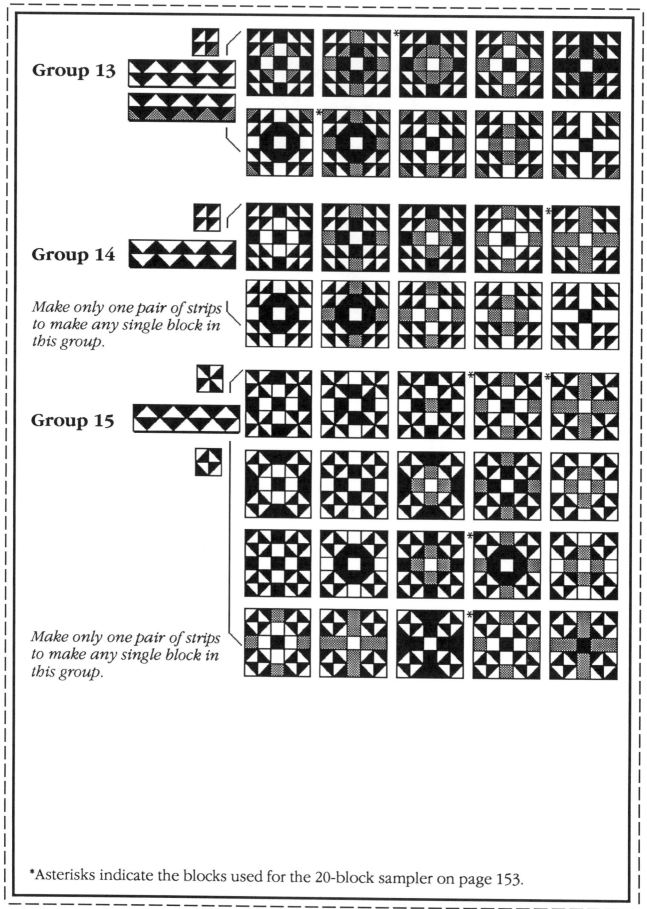

Group 13

Group 14

Make only one pair of strips to make any single block in this group.

Group 15

Make only one pair of strips to make any single block in this group.

*Asterisks indicate the blocks used for the 20-block sampler on page 153.

A twenty-block sampler

If made from 5" Alpha strips with borders as shown, this project will be about 64" x 78". (Use 3-1/2 yds. for backing. No other yardage is given since you can have so many combinations of fabrics.)

1. Cut assorted Alpha strips, an even number from each fabric. Total needed: 16 **lights,** 14 **darks,** six **mediums.**

2. Make 4 x 4 checker-boards, two fabrics in each: five **dark/ light** combinations, one **dark/ medium** combination, and three **light/medium.**

3. Turn on the bias, mark centers, and cut into strips.

4. Make Beta strips (same or new fabrics: three from **medium,** three from **dark,** two from **light.**)

5. Make panels shown below (notice group numbers).

6. Add 80 bars and **20 centers** (choose the prettiest combinations for each block).

7. Make blocks marked with asterisks or others from those groups.

Group 1

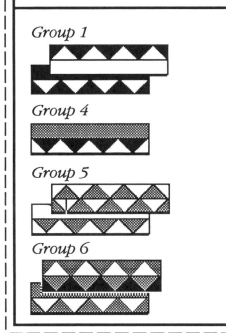

Group 4

Group 5

Group 6

Group 8

Group 10

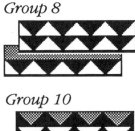

Group 11

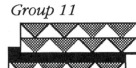

Group 13

Group 14

Group 15

Five-Patch wall hangings

Several beautiful Five-Patch wall hangings are shown in the color section. Here are some ideas for designing your own. (Also see page 141.)

Add a sawtooth border.

The blue and white project in Color Plate 19 uses a sawtooth border around four Crown of Thorns blocks; you can use any Five-Patch block. Make a 4 x 8 checkerboard using the same size Alpha strips as used for the blocks. Read Chapter 6 for the technique, and make Size 3 on the sawtooth chart on page 98.

Note: *With an even number of triangles on borders, but an odd number of units in the design (5 + 5 + 1 for sashing), triangles won't line up if you use Beta-width borders. Make sashing and borders narrower (shown here) or wider (right and in Color Plate 19) or use a diagonal set (page 155) to avoid the problem.*

Use novelty sashing.

Can you spot the Pinwheel blocks in the design on Color Plate 3? Designer sashing creates a whole new effect. Don't mess with Pinwheels until you're really sure of yourself. But once you're ready, be prepared for some excitement. (Even then, you may find results are different from those here.) You need 12 fancy sashing strips and nine dark squares.

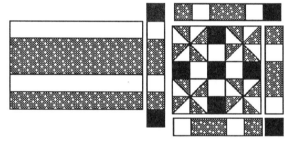

Use strip-piecing to make sashing strips.

Set the blocks diagonally.

This wall hanging uses Spring-field blocks made with 4" Alpha strips and set with designer sash-ing. The project is about 44" square.

Fabric needed:

Light: 1/2 yd.

Medium: 1/3 yd.

Dark: 2-2/3 yds. (including backing and large background triangles)

Border prints with 4 repeats: 3/4 yd. for inner borders; 1-1/4 yds. for outer borders

Batting: 48" square

1. Cut Alpha strips: six light, eight dark, and two medium.

2. Make checkerboards: a 4 x 4 from dark and medium, a 4 x 4 from dark and light, and a 4 x 8 from dark and light.

3. Turn small checkerboards on the bias, mark centers, and cut strips of triangles.

4. Cut Beta strips: two each of medium and light, and three of dark fabric.

5. Make four Springfield B blocks, page 166. (Save the left-over strip of triangles in case you need it for the sawtooth borders.)

6. Make novelty sashing. Piece these together individually since only four strips are needed and you may want to use carefully selected border sections. Cut four strips of dark fabric, Beta width and 6-1/2" long. Cut eight squares of medium fabric, Beta width. Piece together.

7. Assemble four blocks, add-ing a single light square in the center. **Add border.**

8. Make sawtooth chains from the 4 x 8 checkerboard as directed in Chapter 6. These will be Size 3 on the chart on page 98. Add 4" strips to the light end.

9 . Make large background triangles. Cut two 17" squares of dark fabric. Cut diagonally. **As-semble** as shown on the bottom of page 93.

10. Add more borders as de-sired. (Keep size under 44" square to fit backing.)

11. Add backing from remaining dark fabric. **Quilt and bind as desired.**

More ideas for designing your own Five-Patch projects

Make a two-color quilt.

Many projects (including sampler quilts) can be made with just two colors. Here are calculations for a 16-block quilt about 65" square from 5" Alpha strips. Cut Alpha strips cross-grain. Divide remaining fabric lengthwise for Beta strips, sashing, borders, etc.

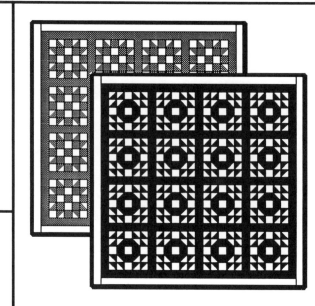

Fabric needed:

Dominant color: (color used for sashing): 3-1/2 yds.

Second color: 3 yds.

Backing: 3-1/2 yds.

Set blocks diagonally.

Here's how some of the Five-Patch blocks look set on point. Fool's Square is especially interesting when set this way.

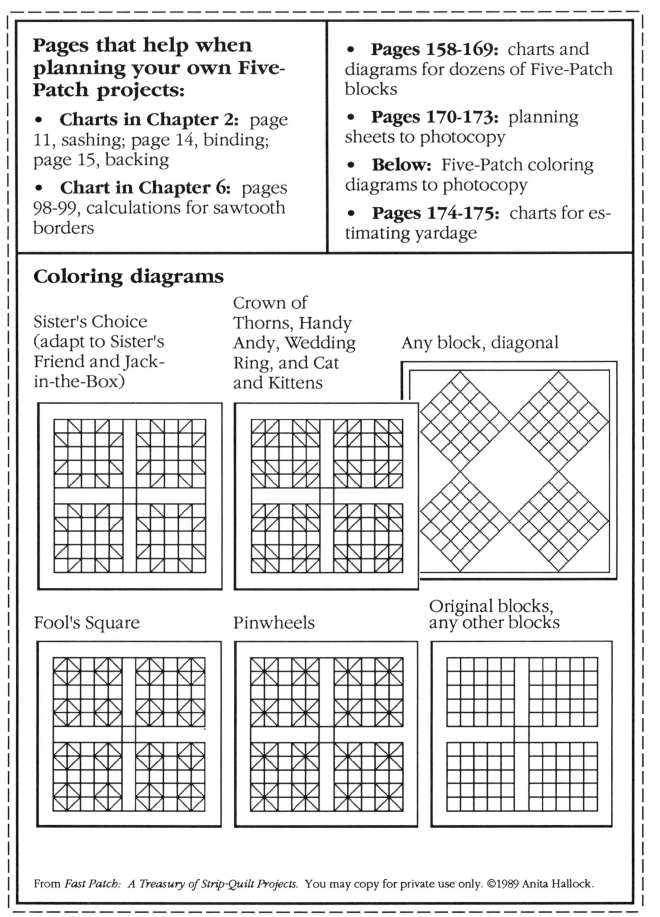

Pages that help when planning your own Five-Patch projects:

- **Charts in Chapter 2:** page 11, sashing; page 14, binding; page 15, backing

- **Chart in Chapter 6:** pages 98-99, calculations for sawtooth borders

- **Pages 158-169:** charts and diagrams for dozens of Five-Patch blocks

- **Pages 170-173:** planning sheets to photocopy

- **Below:** Five-Patch coloring diagrams to photocopy

- **Pages 174-175:** charts for estimating yardage

Coloring diagrams

Sister's Choice (adapt to Sister's Friend and Jack-in-the-Box)

Crown of Thorns, Handy Andy, Wedding Ring, and Cat and Kittens

Any block, diagonal

Fool's Square

Pinwheels

Original blocks, any other blocks

From *Fast Patch: A Treasury of Strip-Quilt Projects.* You may copy for private use only. ©1989 Anita Hallock.

Five-Patch charts

Sister's Choice A

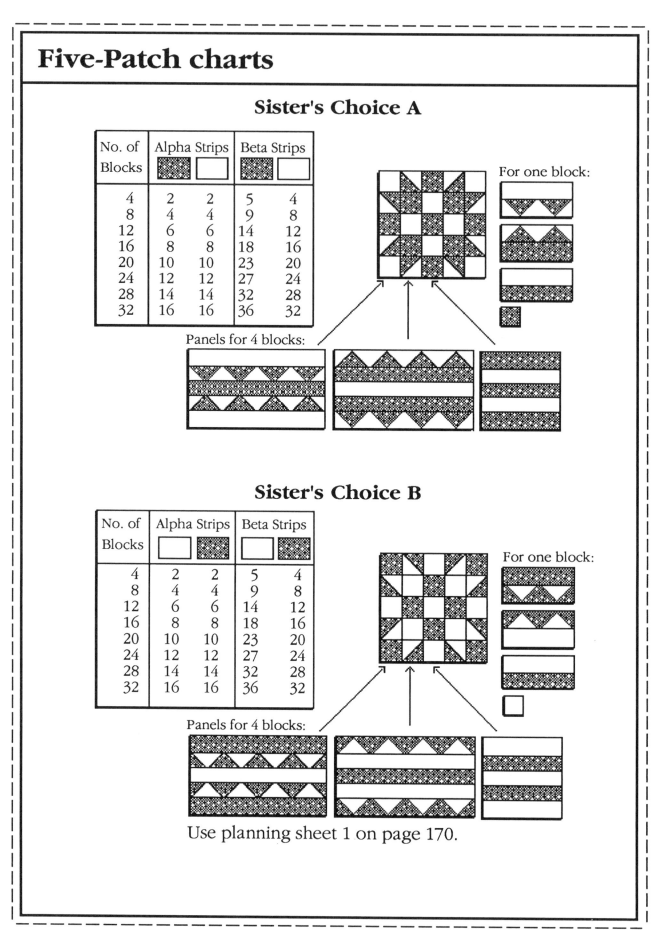

No. of Blocks	Alpha Strips		Beta Strips	
4	2	2	5	4
8	4	4	9	8
12	6	6	14	12
16	8	8	18	16
20	10	10	23	20
24	12	12	27	24
28	14	14	32	28
32	16	16	36	32

For one block:

Panels for 4 blocks:

Sister's Choice B

No. of Blocks	Alpha Strips		Beta Strips	
4	2	2	5	4
8	4	4	9	8
12	6	6	14	12
16	8	8	18	16
20	10	10	23	20
24	12	12	27	24
28	14	14	32	28
32	16	16	36	32

For one block:

Panels for 4 blocks:

Use planning sheet 1 on page 170.

Sister's Choice C

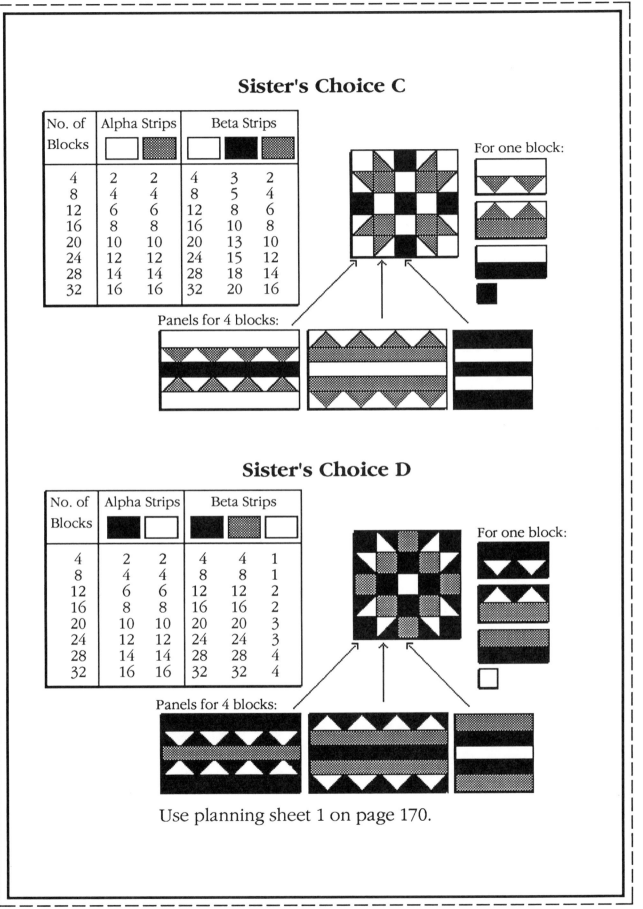

No. of Blocks	Alpha Strips		Beta Strips		
	☐	▓	☐	■	▓
4	2	2	4	3	2
8	4	4	8	5	4
12	6	6	12	8	6
16	8	8	16	10	8
20	10	10	20	13	10
24	12	12	24	15	12
28	14	14	28	18	14
32	16	16	32	20	16

For one block:

Panels for 4 blocks:

Sister's Choice D

No. of Blocks	Alpha Strips		Beta Strips		
	■	☐	■	▓	☐
4	2	2	4	4	1
8	4	4	8	8	1
12	6	6	12	12	2
16	8	8	16	16	2
20	10	10	20	20	3
24	12	12	24	24	3
28	14	14	28	28	4
32	16	16	32	32	4

For one block:

Panels for 4 blocks:

Use planning sheet 1 on page 170.

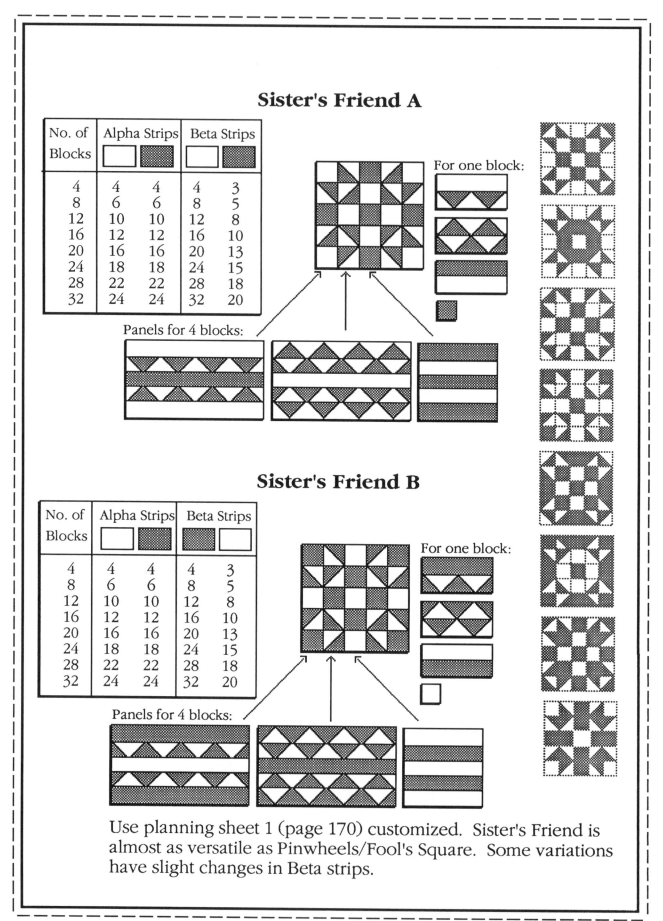

Sister's Friend A

No. of Blocks	Alpha Strips		Beta Strips	
4	4	4	4	3
8	6	6	8	5
12	10	10	12	8
16	12	12	16	10
20	16	16	20	13
24	18	18	24	15
28	22	22	28	18
32	24	24	32	20

For one block:

Panels for 4 blocks:

Sister's Friend B

No. of Blocks	Alpha Strips		Beta Strips	
4	4	4	4	3
8	6	6	8	5
12	10	10	12	8
16	12	12	16	10
20	16	16	20	13
24	18	18	24	15
28	22	22	28	18
32	24	24	32	20

For one block:

Panels for 4 blocks:

Use planning sheet 1 (page 170) customized. Sister's Friend is almost as versatile as Pinwheels/Fool's Square. Some variations have slight changes in Beta strips.

Sister's Friend C

No. of Blocks	Alpha Strips			Beta Strips		
4	2	4	2	4	2	1
8	4	6	2	8	4	1
12	6	10	4	12	6	2
16	8	12	4	16	8	2
20	10	16	6	20	10	3
24	12	18	6	24	12	3
28	14	22	8	28	14	4
32	16	24	8	32	16	4

For one block:

Panels for 4 blocks:

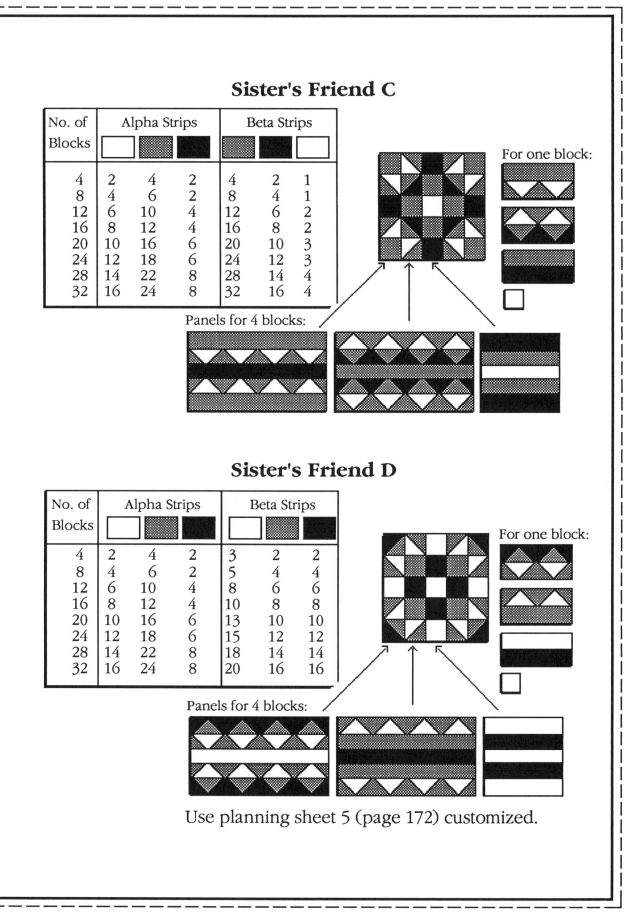

Sister's Friend D

No. of Blocks	Alpha Strips			Beta Strips		
4	2	4	2	3	2	2
8	4	6	2	5	4	4
12	6	10	4	8	6	6
16	8	12	4	10	8	8
20	10	16	6	13	10	10
24	12	18	6	15	12	12
28	14	22	8	18	14	14
32	16	24	8	20	16	16

For one block:

Panels for 4 blocks:

Use planning sheet 5 (page 172) customized.

Crown of Thorns A

No. of Blocks	Alpha Strips		Beta Strips	
	☐	▨	☐	▨
4	4	4	3	2
8	8	8	5	4
12	12	12	8	6
16	16	16	10	8
20	20	20	13	10
24	24	24	15	12
28	28	28	18	14
32	32	32	20	16

For one block:

Panels for 4 blocks:

Crown of Thorns B

No. of Blocks	Alpha Strips		Beta Strips	
	▨	☐	▨	☐
4	4	4	3	2
8	8	8	5	4
12	12	12	8	6
16	16	16	10	8
20	20	20	13	10
24	24	24	15	12
28	28	28	18	14
32	32	32	20	16

For one block:

Panels for 4 blocks:

Use planning sheet 4 on page 172.

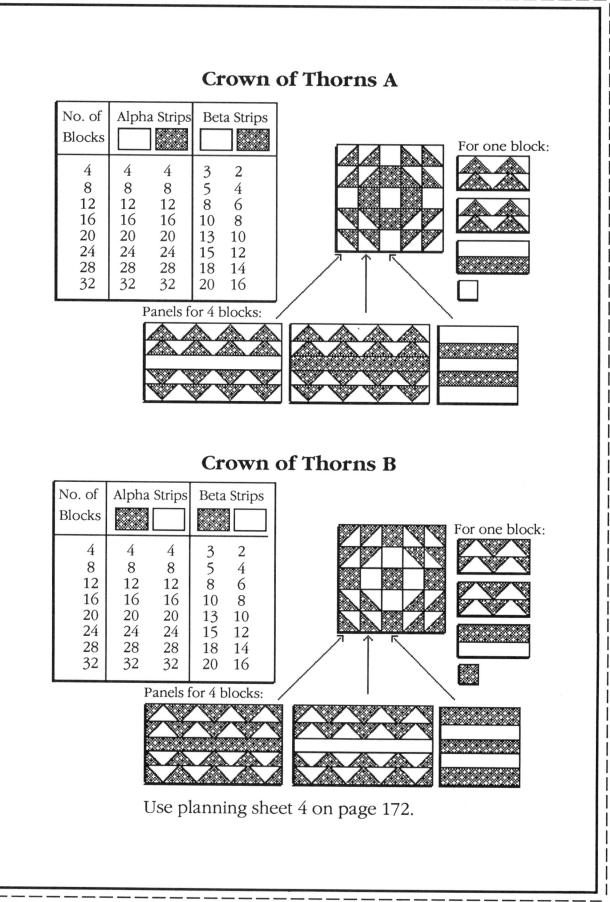

Crown of Thorns C

No. of Blocks	Alpha Strips			Beta Strips	
4	4	6	2	3	2
8	6	8	2	5	4
12	10	14	4	8	6
16	12	16	4	10	8
20	16	22	6	13	10
24	18	24	6	15	12
28	22	30	8	18	14
32	24	32	8	20	16

For one block:

Panels for 4 blocks:

Crown of Thorns D

No. of Blocks	Alpha Strips			Beta Strips	
4	4	6	2	3	2
8	6	8	2	5	4
12	10	14	4	8	6
16	12	16	4	10	8
20	16	22	6	13	10
24	18	24	6	15	12
28	22	30	8	18	14
32	24	32	8	20	16

For one block:

Panels for 4 blocks:

Use planning sheet 4 on page 172.

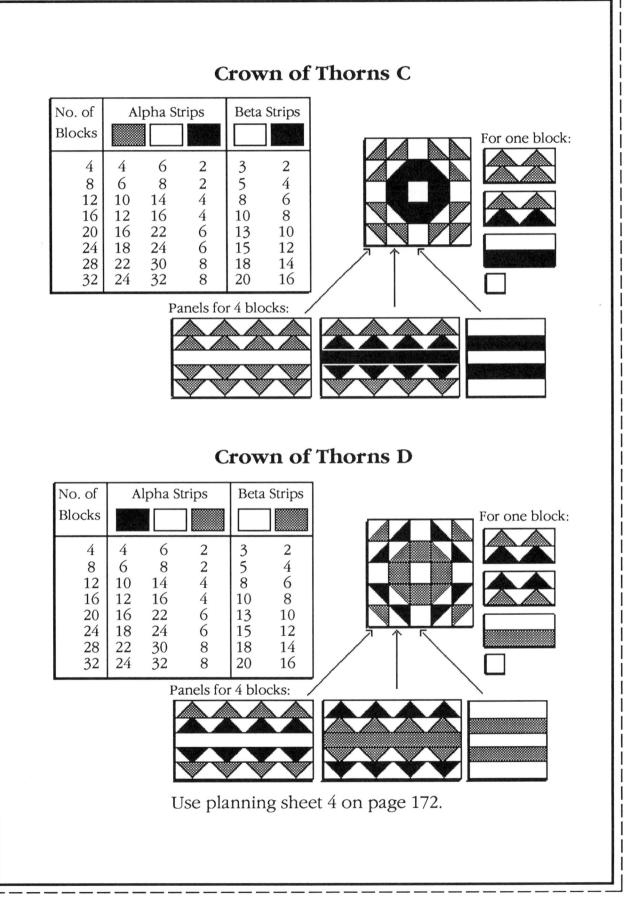

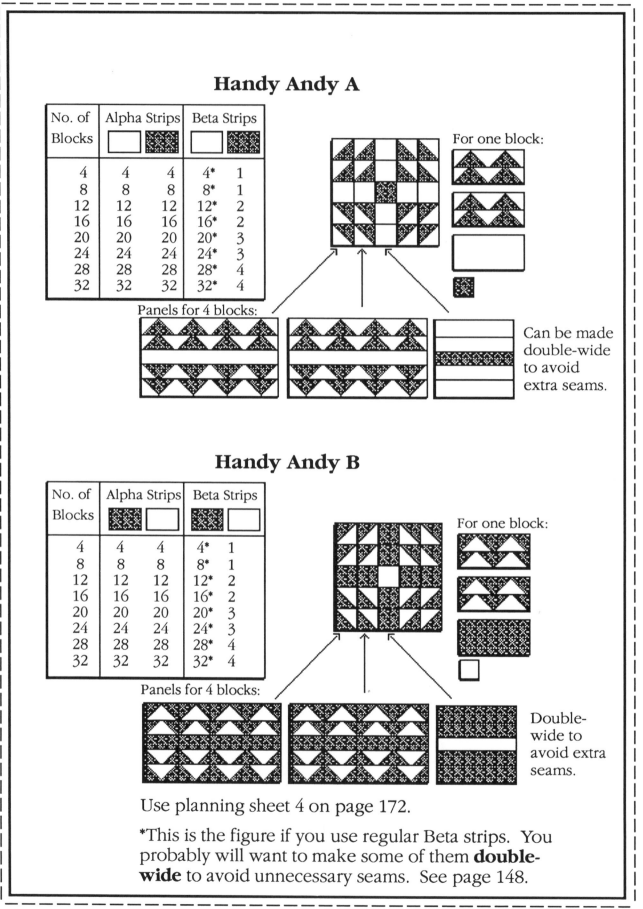

Handy Andy A

No. of Blocks	Alpha Strips		Beta Strips	
4	4	4	4*	1
8	8	8	8*	1
12	12	12	12*	2
16	16	16	16*	2
20	20	20	20*	3
24	24	24	24*	3
28	28	28	28*	4
32	32	32	32*	4

For one block:

Panels for 4 blocks:

Can be made double-wide to avoid extra seams.

Handy Andy B

No. of Blocks	Alpha Strips		Beta Strips	
4	4	4	4*	1
8	8	8	8*	1
12	12	12	12*	2
16	16	16	16*	2
20	20	20	20*	3
24	24	24	24*	3
28	28	28	28*	4
32	32	32	32*	4

For one block:

Panels for 4 blocks:

Double-wide to avoid extra seams.

Use planning sheet 4 on page 172.

*This is the figure if you use regular Beta strips. You probably will want to make some of them **double-wide** to avoid unnecessary seams. See page 148.

Memory Wreath A

No. of Blocks	Alpha Strips		Beta Strips		
	⬜	▨	▨	⬜	▨
4	4	4	4	2	1
8	6	6	8	4	1
12	10	10	12	6	2
16	12	12	16	8	2
20	16	16	20	10	3
24	18	18	24	12	3
28	22	22	28	14	4
32	24	24	32	16	4

For one block:

Panels for 4 blocks:

Memory Wreath B

No. of Blocks	Alpha Strips		Beta Strips		
	▨	⬜	▨	▨	⬜
4	4	4	4	2	1
8	6	6	8	4	1
12	10	10	12	6	2
16	12	12	16	8	2
20	16	16	20	10	3
24	18	18	24	12	3
28	22	22	28	14	4
32	24	24	32	16	4

For one block:

Panels for 4 blocks:

Use planning sheet 5 (page 172) customized.

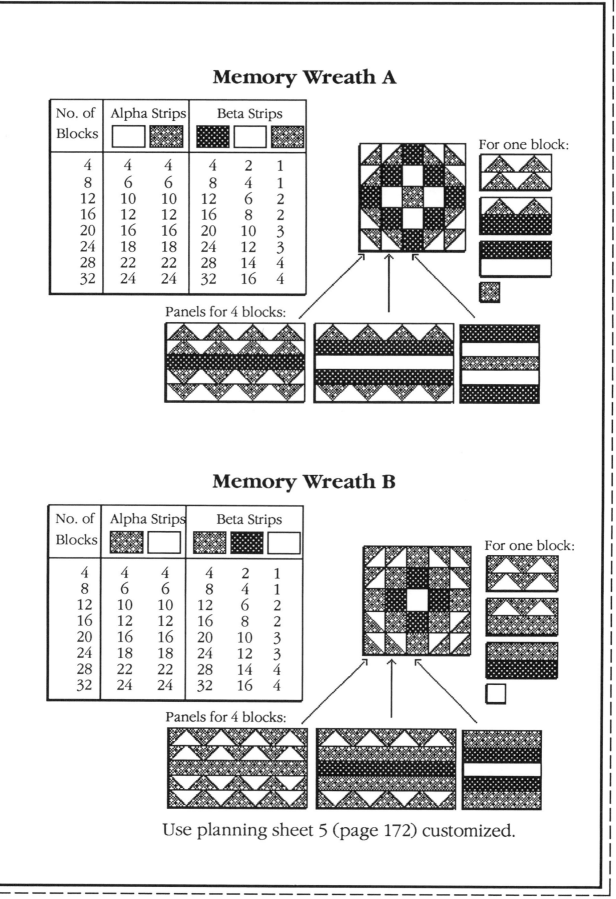

Springfield A

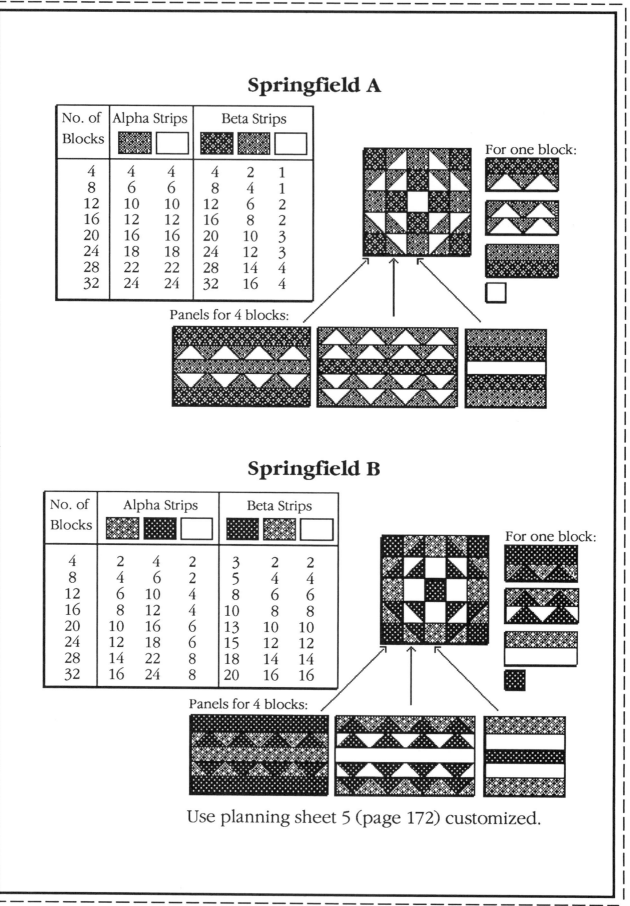

No. of Blocks	Alpha Strips		Beta Strips		
4	4	4	4	2	1
8	6	6	8	4	1
12	10	10	12	6	2
16	12	12	16	8	2
20	16	16	20	10	3
24	18	18	24	12	3
28	22	22	28	14	4
32	24	24	32	16	4

For one block:

Panels for 4 blocks:

Springfield B

No. of Blocks	Alpha Strips			Beta Strips		
4	2	4	2	3	2	2
8	4	6	2	5	4	4
12	6	10	4	8	6	6
16	8	12	4	10	8	8
20	10	16	6	13	10	10
24	12	18	6	15	12	12
28	14	22	8	18	14	14
32	16	24	8	20	16	16

For one block:

Panels for 4 blocks:

Use planning sheet 5 (page 172) customized.

Fool's Square/Pinwheels

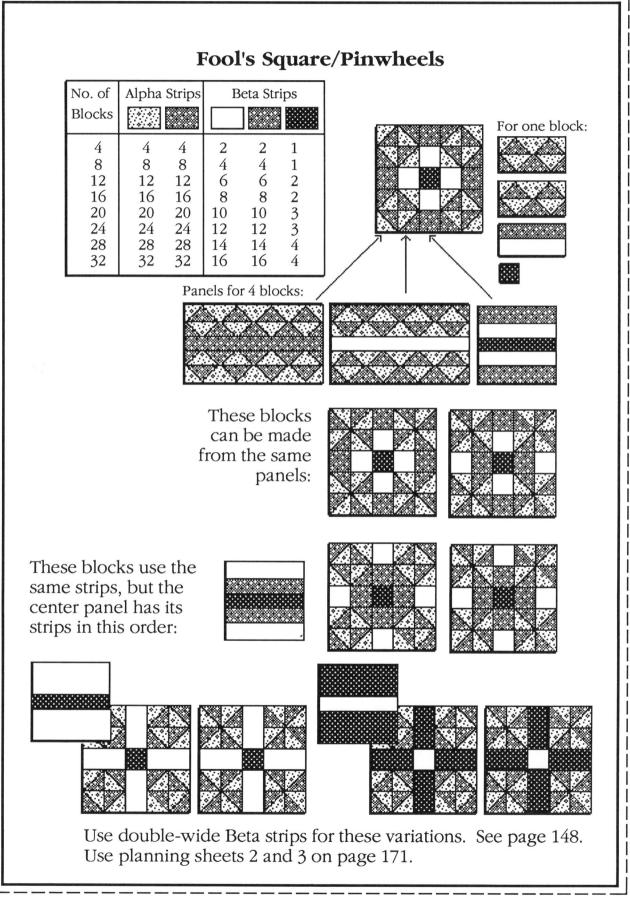

No. of Blocks	Alpha Strips		Beta Strips		
4	4	4	2	2	1
8	8	8	4	4	1
12	12	12	6	6	2
16	16	16	8	8	2
20	20	20	10	10	3
24	24	24	12	12	3
28	28	28	14	14	4
32	32	32	16	16	4

For one block:

Panels for 4 blocks:

These blocks can be made from the same panels:

These blocks use the same strips, but the center panel has its strips in this order:

Use double-wide Beta strips for these variations. See page 148.
Use planning sheets 2 and 3 on page 171.

There are so many Five-Patch blocks that I can't begin to show them all. Here's a quick look at more; many variations can be made for each of these.

Cat and Kittens

No. of Blocks	Alpha Strips			Beta Strips		
4	4	6	2	2	2	1
8	6	8	2	4	4	1
12	10	14	4	6	6	2
16	12	16	4	8	8	2
20	16	22	6	10	10	3
24	18	24	6	12	12	3
28	22	30	8	14	14	4
32	24	32	8	16	16	4

For one block:

Use planning sheet 4 (page 172)

Panels for 4 blocks:

Square Dance

Square Dance is as easy as Sister's Choice to sew, but a pretty block isn't automatic, so be careful with colors.

No. of Blocks	Alpha Strips		Beta Strips			
4	2	2	4	2	2	1
8	4	4	8	4	4	1
12	6	6	12	6	6	2
16	8	8	16	8	8	2
20	10	10	20	10	10	3
24	12	12	24	12	12	3
28	14	14	28	14	14	4
32	16	16	32	16	16	4

For one block:

Panels for 4 blocks:

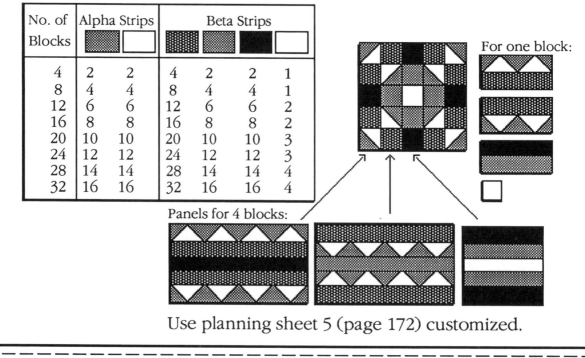

Use planning sheet 5 (page 172) customized.

Two advanced blocks

These aren't for beginners. Jack-in-the-Box can drive you crazy. Panels are tricky and half the blocks revolve in one direction, half in the other. Two separate quilts were made for Color Plate 5.

Jack-in-the-Box

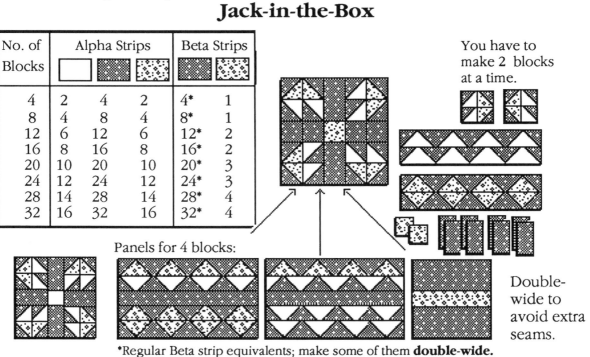

No. of Blocks	Alpha Strips			Beta Strips	
4	2	4	2	4*	1
8	4	8	4	8*	1
12	6	12	6	12*	2
16	8	16	8	16*	2
20	10	20	10	20*	3
24	12	24	12	24*	3
28	14	28	14	28*	4
32	16	32	16	32*	4

You have to make 2 blocks at a time.

Double-wide to avoid extra seams.

Panels for 4 blocks:

*Regular Beta strip equivalents; make some of them **double-wide**. (See page 148.)

Wedding Ring

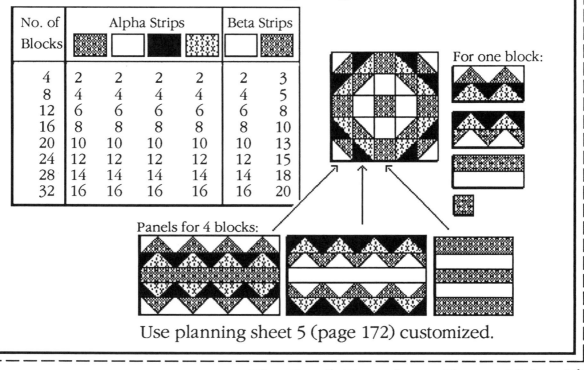

No. of Blocks	Alpha Strips				Beta Strips	
4	2	2	2	2	2	3
8	4	4	4	4	4	5
12	6	6	6	6	6	8
16	8	8	8	8	8	10
20	10	10	10	10	10	13
24	12	12	12	12	12	15
28	14	14	14	14	14	18
32	16	16	16	16	16	20

For one block:

Panels for 4 blocks:

Use planning sheet 5 (page 172) customized.

Five-Patch planning sheets

These planning sheets help translate the black-and-white art work to your fabric.

Use them any way you want; here's one way you might proceed.

1. Decide on your block. Make several copies of the coloring sheets on page 157 and the planning sheet for that block.

2. Make a tentative choice of fabric. If you're at a store, get tiny samples of actual fabric to take home, if possible.

3. Color in the several coloring sheets (including borders, etc.) with colored pencils to find a nice combination. To avoid confusion, have colors match the darks and lights in the diagrams on pages 158 to 169, especially for your first project.

4. Transfer your color scheme to the planning sheet for your block.

5. Fill in information about block sizes, number of strips needed, etc.

6. Calculate the yardage you need (using the charts on pages 174-175). Write the total by the box representing that fabric.

7. Take the diagrams to the store when you purchase the fabric.

8. Attach diagrams to the book page or sewing machine for handy reference.

1. Sister's Choice Planning Sheet

Block and variation _____ Block size ___ Number of blocks ___

	Alpha Strips		Beta Strips		
No. of Strips					
Size of Strips					

Yardage needed

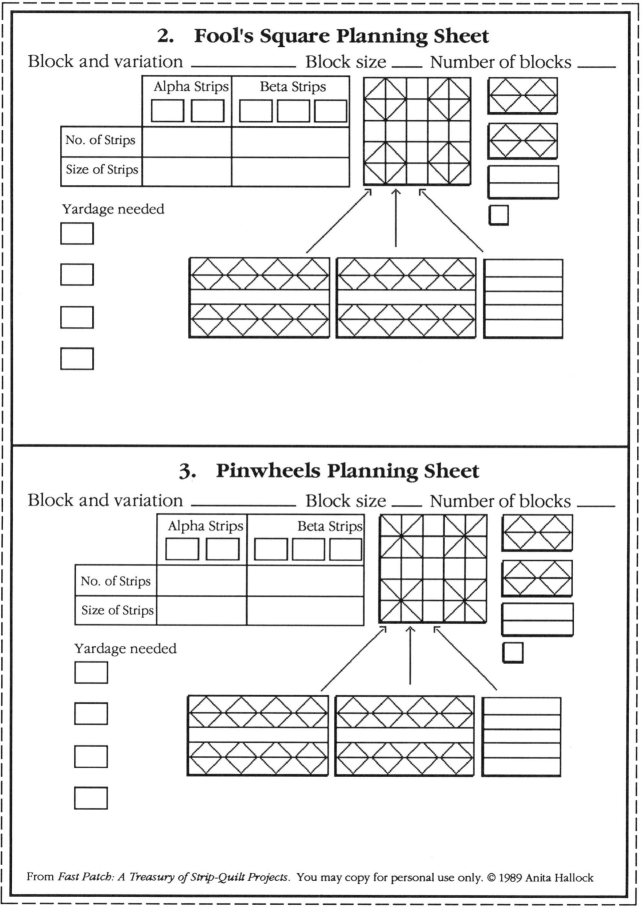

2. Fool's Square Planning Sheet

Block and variation _____ Block size ____ Number of blocks ____

	Alpha Strips		Beta Strips		
	☐	☐	☐	☐	☐
No. of Strips					
Size of Strips					

Yardage needed

☐

☐

☐

☐

3. Pinwheels Planning Sheet

Block and variation _____ Block size ____ Number of blocks ____

	Alpha Strips		Beta Strips		
	☐	☐	☐	☐	☐
No. of Strips					
Size of Strips					

Yardage needed

☐

☐

☐

☐

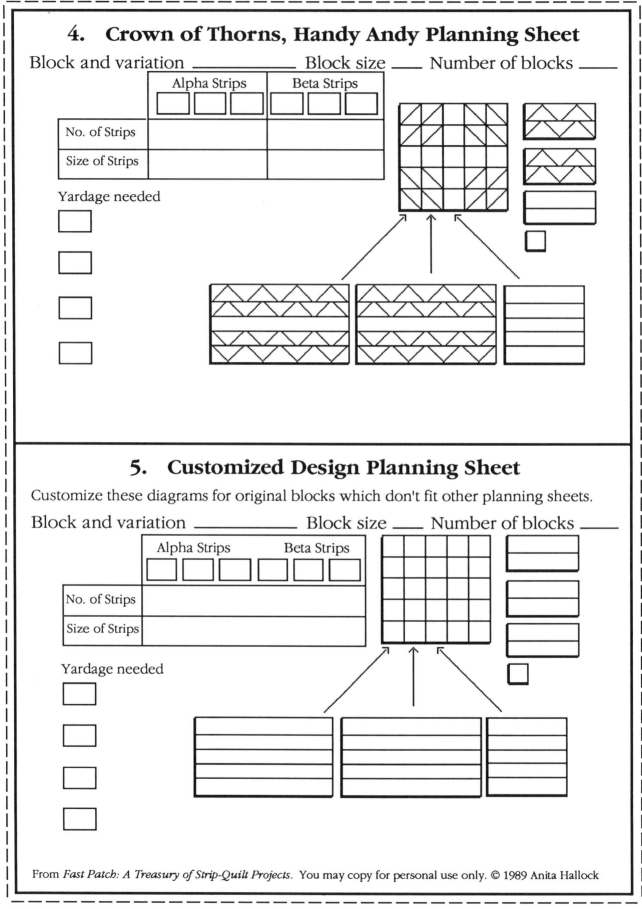

4. Crown of Thorns, Handy Andy Planning Sheet

Block and variation _____ Block size ___ Number of blocks ___

	Alpha Strips			Beta Strips		
No. of Strips						
Size of Strips						

Yardage needed

5. Customized Design Planning Sheet

Customize these diagrams for original blocks which don't fit other planning sheets.

Block and variation _____ Block size ___ Number of blocks ___

	Alpha Strips			Beta Strips		
No. of Strips						
Size of Strips						

Yardage needed

Appendix

Sizes of final triangles

Triangles will be this size after cutting and 1/4" seam allowances. Original strip size is at the bottom of each square.

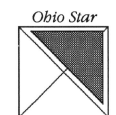

Ohio Star

All others

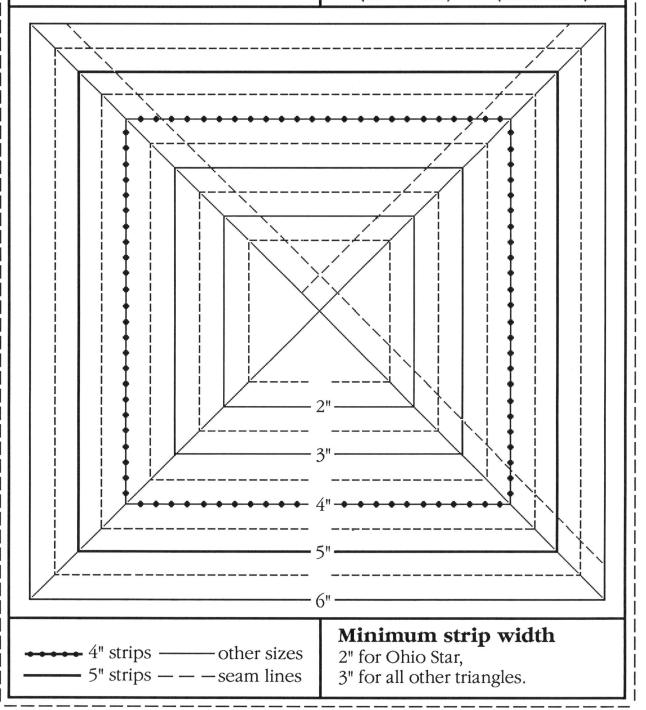

2"

3"

4"

5"

6"

•—•—•—• 4" strips ———— other sizes

———— 5" strips — — — seam lines

Minimum strip width
2" for Ohio Star,
3" for all other triangles.

Yardage for blocks and sawtooth chains, Chapters 6, 7, and 8

Projects with 4" x 17" Alpha strips

The symbol > means cut with the grain (parallel to selvage); ∧ means cut across the grain.
The first chart gives **Alpha strips**.

Strips	Yardage	Strips	Yardage	Strips	Yardage
8	1/2 yd ∧	18	1-1/8 yd ∧ or 1 yd >	28	1-2/3 yd ∧ or 1-1/2 yd >
10	2/3 yd ∧	20	1-1/4 yd ∧ or 1 yd >	30	1-3/4 yd ∧ or 1-1/2 yd >
12	3/4 yd ∧	22	1-1/3 yd ∧	32	1-7/8 yd ∧
14	1 yd ∧	24	1-1/2 yd∧		
16	1 yd∧ or >	26	1-1/2 yd ∧ or >		

The next chart gives **Beta strips** to match (about 2-1/2" x 20"). Cut across grain (two across).

Strips	Yardage	Strips	Yardage	Strips	Yardage
1-6	1/4 yd	13-18	2/3 yd	25-32	1-1/4 yd
7-8	1/3 yd	19-20	3/4 yd		
9-12	1/2 yd	21-24	1 yd		

Projects with 5" x 21" Alpha strips

Alpha strips are all cut across grain (two across).

Strips	Yardage	Strips	Yardage	Strips	Yardage
8	2/3 yd	18	1-1/3 yd	28	2 yd (if careful)
10	3/4 yd	20	1-1/2 yd	30	2-1/4 yd
12	1 yd	22	1-3/4 yd	32	2-1/3 yd
14	1-1/8 yd	24	1-3/4 yd		
16	1-1/4 yd	26	1-7/8 yd		

Beta strips to match (about 3-1/8" x 25")

You usually share this yardage with borders, etc., and cut all strips the same direction. It's wasteful to cut strips this size across grain unless you remove fabric for borders first. Here's yardage if you are cutting *only* Beta strips.

Strips	Yardage	Strips	Yardage	Strips	Yardage
1-2	1/4 yd ∧	8-13	3/4 yd >	27-28	1-2/3 yd ∧ and >
3	1/3 yd ∧	14-15	1 yd ∧ and >	29-30	1-3/4 yd ∧ and >
4-5	1/2 yd ∧	16-18	1-1/4 yd ∧ and >	31-32	2 yd ∧ and >
6-7	2/3 yd ∧	19-26	1-1/2 yd >	32-39	2-1/4 yd >

∧ and > Cut the first 13 or 26 lengthwise, and the rest across grain.

Note: *See page 63 for Two-Color Ohio Star yardage and page 89 for Ohio Star yardage.*

Yardage for completing the basic quilt top

(Also see page 14 for binding yardage and page 15 for backing yardage.)

Yardage for sashing and inner borders

Calculations are for sashing and inner borders of the same fabric, cut the same width.

1. Cut the yardage into equal-width strips (lengthwise, unless less than 1-1/4 yds.) Fold yardage to make two or four layers. Start cuts at edge and work toward fold.

2. Set aside borders and long sashing to avoid cutting accidentally.

3. Cut remaining strips into short sashing, same length as blocks. (See chart on page 11 for number.) If you need more, cut from ends of strips set aside in Step 2.

Blocks Used	Small Blocks (9"-10")		Large Blocks (12"-13")		
	Width of Sashing		Width of Sashing		
	2-1/2" (17*)	3" (14*)	3" (14*)	3-1/2" (12*)	4" (11+)
9 (3 x 3)	2/3 yd	3/4 yd	3/4 yd	1-1/2 yd	1-1/2 yd
12 (3 x 4)	2/3 yd	3/4 yd	1 yd	1-2/3 yd	1-3/4 yd
15 (3 x 5)	7/8 yd	1 yd	1-1/2 yd	1-2/3 yd	2-1/4 yd
16 (4 x 4)	1-1/2 yd	1-1/2 yd	2 yd	2 yd	2 yd
20 (4 x 5)	1-1/2 yd	1-1/2 yd	2-1/8 yd	2-1/8 yd	2-1/3 yd
24 (4 x 6)	1-1/2 yd	1-2/3 yd	2 yd	2-2/3 yd	3 yd
25 (5 x 5)	1-3/4 yd	2 yd	2-1/4 yd	2-1/3 yd	3-1/8 yd
30 (5 x 6)	2 yd	2-1/8 yd	2-1/2 yd	2-2/3 yd	3-1/3 yd
36 (6 x 6)	2-1/4 yd	2-1/3 yd	2-2/3 yd	3-1/8 yd	3-3/4 yd
42 (6 x 7)	2-1/3 yd	2-1/2 yd	3-1/8 yd	3-1/2 yd	4 yd

* You can cut this many strips lengthwise from 44" fabric.

+ Make a bit narrower if necessary.

Yardage for plain blocks

Use this instead of the chart above if you alternate patchwork with plain blocks.

Block Size:	7"- 8"	8"-10"	11"-12"	13"-14"
Before seams:	up to 8-3/4" (5 across)	up to 11" (4 across)	up to 12-1/2" (3 across)	up to 14-1/2" (3 across)
Number of blocks and yardage	1-5=1/4 yd 6-10=1/2 yd 11-15=3/4 yd 16-20=1 yd 21-25=1-1/4 yd	1-4=1/3yd 5-8=2/3 yd 9-12=1 yd 13-16=1-1/4 yd 17-20=1-2/3 yd 21-24=2 yd	4-6=1-3/4 yd 7-9=1-1/8 yd 10-12=1-1/2 yd 13-15=1-3/4 yd 16-18=2-1/8 yd 19-21=2-1/2 yd	4-6 =1 yd 7-9 =1-1/4 yd 10-12 =1-2/3 yd 13-15 =2-1/8 yd 16-18 =2-1/2 yd 19-21 =3 yd

Yardage for borders

Cut strips cross-grain, unless you combine yardage with other parts of quilt.

Quilt type (see page 15)	Strips	2-1/2"	3"	3-1/2"	4"
1, Twin throw	7	1/2 yd	2/3 yd	7/8 yd	1 yd
2 or 3, Twin spread, double cover, queen throw	8	2/3 yd	3/4 yd	1 yd	1 yd
4 or 5, Double spread, queen cover, king throw	9	2/3 yd	7/8 yd	1 yd	1-1/4 yd
6 or 7, Queen or king spread	10	3/4 yd	1 yd	1 yd	1-1/4 yd

Common sizes of checkerboards and what they look like turned on the bias

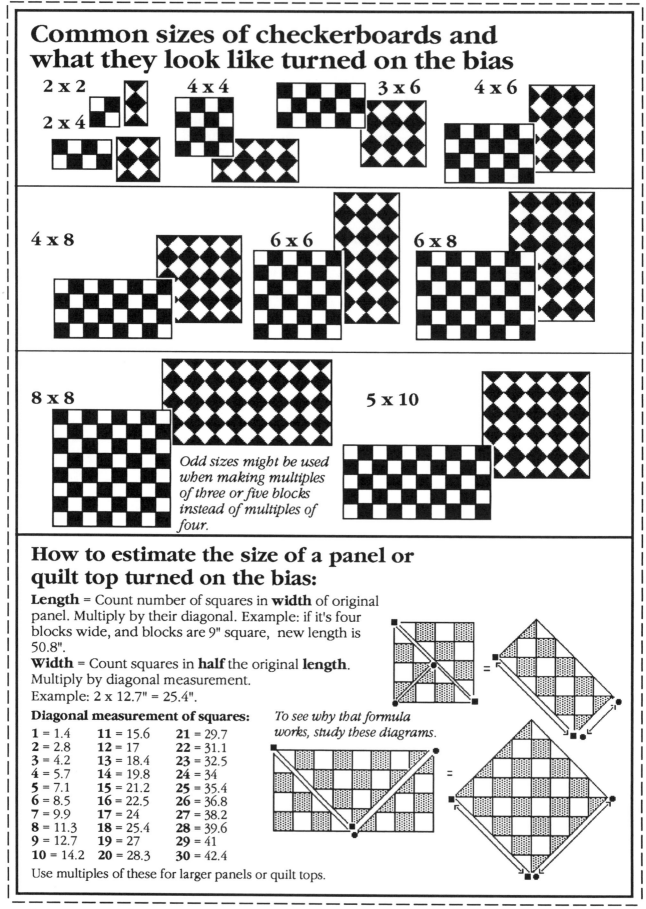

2 x 2

2 x 4

4 x 4

3 x 6

4 x 6

4 x 8

6 x 6

6 x 8

8 x 8

5 x 10

Odd sizes might be used when making multiples of three or five blocks instead of multiples of four.

How to estimate the size of a panel or quilt top turned on the bias:

Length = Count number of squares in **width** of original panel. Multiply by their diagonal. Example: if it's four blocks wide, and blocks are 9" square, new length is 50.8".

Width = Count squares in **half** the original **length**. Multiply by diagonal measurement.
Example: 2 x 12.7" = 25.4".

To see why that formula works, study these diagrams.

Diagonal measurement of squares:

1 = 1.4	**11** = 15.6	**21** = 29.7
2 = 2.8	**12** = 17	**22** = 31.1
3 = 4.2	**13** = 18.4	**23** = 32.5
4 = 5.7	**14** = 19.8	**24** = 34
5 = 7.1	**15** = 21.2	**25** = 35.4
6 = 8.5	**16** = 22.5	**26** = 36.8
7 = 9.9	**17** = 24	**27** = 38.2
8 = 11.3	**18** = 25.4	**28** = 39.6
9 = 12.7	**19** = 27	**29** = 41
10 = 14.2	**20** = 28.3	**30** = 42.4

Use multiples of these for larger panels or quilt tops.

Cut-apart checkerboard

You can photocopy this page and cut different sizes of checkerboards from this large one. Turn them on the bias, using scissors and removable Scotch tape.

If you start on the bias and "turn on the straight"

With Fast Patch, you have bias on the edge of the block. If this bothers you, make the Alpha strips on the bias. Then when you turn the checkerboard on the diagonal, the grain of the fabric is in the traditional position. It's more wasteful of fabric and harder to calculate the yardage needed. Layouts shown are for 4" x 17" strips.

Fabric needed:

- **3" x 13" strips:** 12" square for first strip; 4-1/2" for each additional.
- **4" x 17" strips:** 15" square for first strip; 6" for each additional strip.
- **5" x 21" strips:** 19" square for first strip; 7" for each additional strip.
- **6" x 25" strips:** 22" for first; 8-1/2" for each additional strip.

15'

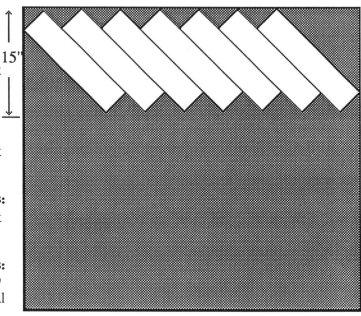

15"

Use the 45° angle mark on your ruler for accurate cutting. Cut through both light and dark fabric at the same time, right sides together.

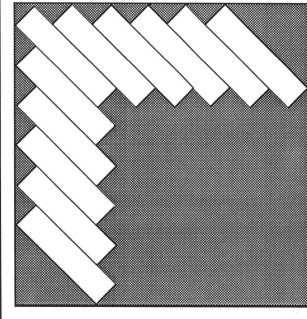

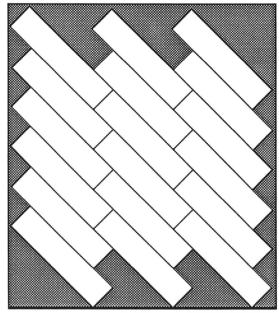

Suggestions for teachers

Make decisions.

There are a lot of projects in this book. Many folks just wouldn't know where to start.

Study page 4. Pick the project you think will match your students' ability and interest. (It's also important that the project be interesting to *you*. An enthusiastic teacher is the single most important factor.) Try to arrange it so the only decision the student makes is which fabrics to use.

By the way, your decision might be that the projects you found fascinating would be too advanced or baffling for the group you have in mind. Consider presenting an informational program instead of a hands-on class. All of the photographs in this book and many more have been assembled into a slide show. Write to the author at Box 2, Springfield, OR, 97477, for information on buying or borrowing the set. It comes with a cassette tape, but it's more effective if you narrate the program yourself, supplementing the slides with your samples.

Make projects.

You need to make at least a couple of samples of whatever you plan to teach to get familiar with any quirks involved. The more times you make up the project yourself, the better you will be able to teach it.

Some projects have a "drop-out" version, a project which stops at the checkerboard stage. If you have a baffled student in with an energetic group doing Ohio Star, it's nice to have an attractive sample of the Ohio Squares (page 69) made up to let her know it's okay to stop at that stage.

Make visual aids.

You must have a set of panels showing steps for making the project. Fast Patch projects are quite indirect and students can't see what they're making until they have it almost done. It really helps if they can see where they're going before they start.

See the summary of strips and panels on pages 47, 103, and 138. You need Steps 5, 6, 9, and 11, at least, and preferably Steps 3, 7, 8, and 10 also. To show how a set of four blocks were made, use enough Alpha strips for 20 blocks and the number of Beta strips indicated for eight blocks. You can leave the panels loose or mount them.

With loose displays, you can put each panel up at the most effective moment, take it to a table for a close-up look, etc. Pin them to a bulletin board or place them onto a flannel board or a layer of batting.

With mounted displays, panels can be nicely arranged and labeled and the whole display looks more professional. But it's more time-consuming to prepare displays this way and you may not be able to remove the panels and make them into a quilt later. Another disadvantage is that you can't remove one panel to discuss the seams on the back or take it to a table to show someone.

Color Plate 2 shows a nifty accordian-fold display. You can reveal one section at a time, or you can show the whole process by spreading out the display. It can be freestanding on a large table, or it can be hung with hooks through the reinforced holes at the top. Panels are based on 4" strips, and the display uses 22" x 28" heavy poster board.

Make room.

Don't try to teach Fast Patch in too small of a room. Fast Patch takes a little more room than traditional patchwork because you're working with panels, not building little chains of patches. It would be nice if each student had a whole table with plenty of room to spread out fabric and leave it stacked for later cutting sessions and to spread out panels to examine them. But that's not practical in a class. You might have three people with their machines share a table, with the rest of the table as a common area for making cuts. You might also have a couple of separate counters or tables (in the adjoining room if necessary) devoted to cutting. You'll need an iron and ironing board of some sort for every four people.

Make the book come to life.

People who study books methodically don't need classes. Although I've worked hard to make this book concise and readable, people will ask you questions rather than looking for the answer in the book. If you are familiar with key pages you can have your students put markers there and turn to the pages for answers. (See pages 104 and 139 for lists of key pages.)

Make sure everyone feels successful.

Every craft has right and wrong ways to do things. Too many warnings ahead of time make us reluctant to try something at all, and mistakes send us back to safe, old techniques. But success at one project brings confidence that carries over to the next. Your job is to help build the confidence.

Since Fast Patch is so different, students don't always know if they're doing a step right or not. By making the project several times yourself, you can warn students (just as they *approach* a pitfall), show the panels made by the faster students to help guide the others, and reassure folks whose work doesn't quite look like the pictures. Look at pages 78 to 80 and 106 to see what I mean.

The first "strange" step is turning the checkerboard on the bias. I usually have everyone watch while the first student makes the bias cuts as I "hold her hand." Other teachers tell me that they have the faster students stop when they complete the checkerboard to wait for the others. Then all students do this step at the same time. (You might not be able to do this if space is limited and folks are sharing the same cutting boards.)

These are just some brief suggestions. Please write to me for more information and for teaching aids if you plan to teach. And please pass on suggestions from your own teaching experience.

Remember, your own personal enthusiasm and experience with the method are your best teaching aids. Good luck.

Recommended reading

For more Fast Patch projects:

Write to Anita Hallock, Box 2, Springfield, OR, 97477 for a listing of publications currently available.

For an overall guide to quiltmaking by machine:

Fanning, Robbie and Tony. *The Complete Book of Machine Quilting*. Radnor, PA: Chilton Book Co., 1980.

For more strip piecing ideas:

Burns, Eleanor. *Quilt in a Day, 1979; Lover's Knot, 1985.* San Marcos, CA: Quilt in a Day.

Johannah, Barbara, *Quick Quiltmaking Handbook*, Menlo Park, CA: Pride of the Forest, 1980.

Olson, Beckie. *Quilts by the Slice.* Lexington, KY: Quilter's Square, 1987.

Young, Blanche and Helen, *Trip Around the World Quilts*, Lafayette, CA: C & T Publishing, 1980.

For quilting and binding:

Dietrich, Mimi, *Happy Endings,* Bothell, WA: That Patchwork Place, 1987.

Johannah, Barbara, *Continuous Curve Quilting*, Menlo Park, CA: Pride of the Forest, 1980.

Hargrave, Harriet. *Heirloom Machine Quilting,* Westminster, CA: Yours Truly, Burdett Design Studios, 1987.

Thompson, Shirley. *Finishing Touches,* and *It's Not a Quilt Until It's Quilted,* Edmonds, WA: Powell Publications, 1980.

For blocks which can be adapted to the Fast Patch technique:

Hopkins, Mary Ellen, *It's Okay If You Sit On My Quilt,* Westminster, CA: Yours Truly Publications, 1982. (Over 300 blocks in this book can be made with Fast Patch.)

Note: *If you are unable to locate any of these books, write to* **Quilting Books Unlimited**, *1158 Prairie, Aurora, IL 60506.*

INDEX

How to turn a 4 x 4 checkerboard on the bias

This page is repeated for your convenience. You might want to photocopy it and post it over your work space.

1. Cut diagonally from one corner.

2. Move one piece over and sew it to the other side. (Remember, the triangle won't match the square at the circled points.)

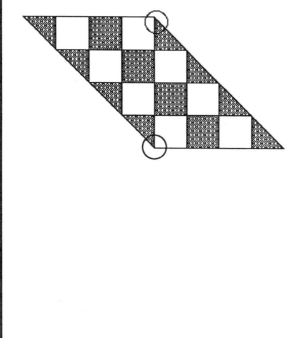

3. Cut diagonally again where the direction changes.

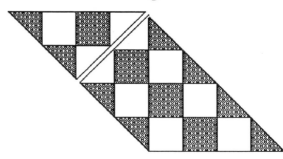

4. Sew the pieces together.

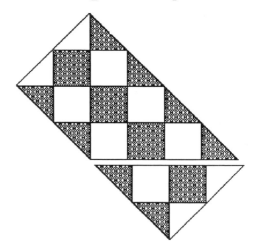